THE GRANDDAUGHTERS
OF IXMUCANÉ

The Granddaughters of Ixmucané

Guatemalan Women Speak

As told to

Emilie Smith-Ayala

Translation by *Emilie Smith-Ayala*

women's
PRESS

CANADIAN CATALOGUING IN PUBLICATION DATA
Smith- Ayala, Emilie
The granddaughters of Ixmucané

ISBN: 0- 88961-169-6

1. Women – Guatemala – Social conditions. 2. Human rights – Guatemala. 3. Women in politics – Guatemala. 4. Women in trade-unions – Guatemala. 5. Women in development – Guatemala. I. Title.

HQ1477.S55   1991   305.42'097281   C91-095099- 7

© copyright 1991 Emilie Smith-Ayala
Editing: P.K. Murphy
Copy editing and proofreading: Margaret Christakos
Cover design: Maresa Masini with the assistance of Sunday Harrison
Cover photograph: The Support Committee for the Internally Displaced People of El Petén

The author would like to thank the Canada Council, Explorations Program, for their support for this project.
Part of the proceeds from the sales of this book will be directed towards a Nuestra Voz sponsored project for the formation of women leaders in the Guatemalan grassroots movement. For more information on this and on other projects, and for on-going information on the situation of women in Guatemala, contact:
Nuestra Voz, A Voice for Guatemalan Women
P.O. Box 20092, 1395 Lawrence Ave W.
Toronto, Ontario,
Canada M6L 1A7

Nuestra Voz, Mujeres de Guatemala
Aptdo. Postal 32–354
México 1 D.F.
C.P. 06030 México

Women's Press gratefully acknowledges the financial support of the Canada Council and the Ontario Arts Council.

Printed and bound in Canada
1 2 3 4 5   1995 1994 1993 1992 1991

Contents

Author's Preface 11
Acknowledgments 12

The Story of Ixmucané 15
Introduction 17
Where the Eyes of the Dead Are Still Watching . . . 17
The Maya 18
The Conquest 18
Colonial Guatemala 20
Post-Independence 22
The Ten Years of Spring 23
Legacy of the Generals 24
Challenging the Generals 27
Military Murderers and Presidential Pirates 27
The Movement Comes Back 29

CHAPTER ONE
Women of the Land 41
We Value Life Very Deeply: Five Centuries of
    Struggle — *Juana Vásquez, Campesino Unity*
    Committee 45
We Believe Refuge Is a Path with an End — *María*
    Teresa Aguilar, Permanent Commission of
    Guatemalan Refugees In Mexico 59
We Are Not the Weaker Sex — *María Celestina*
    Balá, The Campesino Committee of the
    Highlands 68

We've Really Been Able to Resist Everything
— *Paula Carmelita, Communitie of the
Population in Resistance* 73
I Wake Up Early in the Morning, Expecting to See
Him at the Door — *Ana Isabel* 79

CHAPTER TWO

Christian Women Take a Stand 91
I'm a Woman Who Has Touched Reality, Then
Books — *Julia Esquivel* 94
Mary Was Not a Silent Woman — *Sister Eugenia* 102
I'm with My People — *Mother Francisca* 108

CHAPTER THREE

Women in Human Rights Organizations 115
We Aren't Widows — *María Isabel Choxóm
López, Mutual Support Group (GAM)* 119
Every Time I Went Out I Was Followed by
Unidentified Men — *Mercedes Gómez* 125
I Had to Fight for My Sister and Brother
— *Mariela, Runujel Junam Council of Ethnic
Communities (CERJ)* 130
Talking to the Authorities is Like Talking to a
Rock — *Emilia García, Mutual Support Group
(GAM)* 134
Don't Be Fooled by What the President Says
— *Linda Neomí, Mutual Support Group (GAM)* 137
All We Have Now Is a Bitter Memory — *María,
Mutual Support Group (GAM)* 139

CHAPTER FOUR

Women and the Unions 145

My Choice Could Have Been to Serve the System
— *Marta Gloria Torres, United Representation
of the Guatemalan Opposition* 151

This Struggle Isn't Just for Us, It's for Our
Daughters Too — *Rosa Escobar and Carmen
García, The Women's Committee of the
International Union of Food and Allied
Workers' Associations (UITA)* 166

They Can Pay Eight People's Wages by Selling Just
One Skirt — *Patricia, Transcontinental* 171

Someday We're Going to Get What We Want
— *Thelma* 174

CHAPTER FIVE

Women in Women's Organizations 181

You Can't Trade a Husband's Love for a Few
Pounds of Corn — *Rosalina Tuyuc,
Co-ordinator, Board of Directors, Guatemalan
Widows' National Coordinating Group
(CONAVIGUA)* 185

We're Demanding Our Rights, Our Dignity as
Women — *María Morales Jorge, Guatemalan
Widows' National Coordinating Group
(CONAVIGUA)* 191

We Gain Courage from Other Women
— *The Women's Group for the Betterment of the
Family (GRUFEPROMEFAM)* 194

We Can't Isolate Ourselves — *Tierra Viva Women's
Group* 198

CHAPTER SIX

Women in Arms 205

   We Are Not Going to Face Guns with Just Our
      Voices — *Catalina, URNG* 210

   While the Real Power Lies with the Military, There
      Won't Be Any Change — *Judith, URNG* 219

   A Quick Glimpse of Women's Lives in the
      Guatemalan Jungle — *Women from the Rebel
      Armed Forces (FAR), a Member Organization of
      the Guatemalan National Revolutionary Unity
      (URNG)* 225

   I Know Our Struggle is Just and Necessary —
      Laura, URNG 230

   Hope is the Last to Die — *Ines, URNG* 234

Afterword 239

   My Mother Will Be With Us for Hundreds of Years
      — *Rigoberta Menchú, Campesino Unity
      Committee* 239

Notes on Contributors 251

To the memory of my Grandmother, Marjorie Benson;

*To the Grandmothers of my children, Cathleen Smith
and Olga Consuelo Morales Monroy de Ayala;*

*To the memory of my sister-in-law, Beatríz Barrios
Marroquín, murdered by Guatemalan security forces,
between December 10 and 14, 1985.*

Author's Preface

I was born in Argentina, of parents who were born in the United States, and grew up in Canada. But it wasn't until I married a Guatemalan school teacher living in exile in Canada that I found a community.

Creating this book has been a journey towards understanding one of the most painful histories in the Americas. I have spoken with many Guatemalan women, a small number of whose life stories are translated on these pages. It has taken a long time to collect and prepare these narratives, but it has left me a richness that I can only hope others will find as they read this book.

I think the greatest lesson that Guatemalan women can teach us is not to lose faith and hope. In a world where violence, war, environmental devastation and poverty threaten every expression of life and community, where leaders talk chillingly about an all-too-familiar "new world order," these women from their small country in Central America speak with an uncommon wisdom.

I have dedicated this book to a woman who was tortured — her hands cut off — and murdered in Guatemala. Each chapter is dedicated to another woman, who died in a similar way, or who simply disappeared. There are so many, many more. All I can say is that someday we will return and build a monument to them, not a monument to death but one to the towering strength of women.

Emilie Smith-Ayala
August 15, 1991

Acknowledgments

First, I must thank Marta Gloria Torres, whose love I cherish and whose stubborn visionary hope I admire. Max Cabrera Jr. demonstrated moral support, and faith in this project and in my ability to complete it, which pulled me through many a rut. Rosa Escobar and Rodolfo Robles of FESTRAS (formerly UITA–Guatemala) made one of my trips to Guatemala a breeze: finding contacts, arranging meetings, not to mention rocking my baby to sleep and giving me shelter in a tight squeeze. Thanks too to my cousin Sarah Green, who accompanied me on that trip. The women of the international representation of the Campesino Unity Committee in Mexico were also indispensable in helping me make connections, as were the women from the organization Nuestra Voz in Mexico. The women from Nuestra Voz in Canada provided me with support throughout this long process, and the Guatemalan community in exile in Canada has helped me in a thousand ways.

This book would have taken another four years had it not been for the extraordinary babysitting capabilities of my father-in-law, Abel Ayala Peralta, not to mention his help in transcribing several of the interviews. The Ayala-Meza family took my older boys for weeks at a time as I hammered away at the computer keys. Eric and Mynor Ayala also proved wonderful uncles in times of need. My mother-in-law, Cony Ayala, and my parents, Jaime and Cathleen Smith were always strong backers of this project.

The women at Women's Press have been supportive all along, especially Maureen FitzGerald and Angela Robertson.

Editor P.K. Murphy literally transformed my translation, facilitating a much finer book. I must also thank the following religious communities: The Sisters of Saint Joseph, the Ursuline Sisters, and the Sisters of Sion, as well as the Canada Council and the Ontario Arts Council for their financial support.

Finally, I must thank my own family for their patience and support. This project began when I was the mother of one; now I'm the mother of three boys, aged five and under. My children have suffered with me through seventeen-hour bus rides, shoot-outs in Mexican hotels, and evenings on lonely highways in El Quiché, not to mention the hours upon hours I've spent glued to my seat in my closet/office. Abel, Abraham and Axel Balam, thank you boys. To my compañero, Axel, what can I say? It's been hard. We've struggled, but we've always been partners in this work, which goes much further than this book: *Te amaré hasta el fin de los tiempos, y despues, te amaré.*

The Story of Ixmucané[1]

Before the beginning of time, there was nothing but the great darkness above and the endless black ocean below. Then the Sovereign Plumed Serpent moved. Ixmucané, the Grandmother, and Ixpiyacoc, the Grandfather, brought the earth from beneath the waters. The valleys and the mountains appeared. And the land was covered with beautiful forests where giant trees were tied together with tangled vines.

Then they created the animals: deer, birds, snakes, jaguars. They ordered the serpents to be the guardians of the vines and the birds to build their nests in the trees and be the guardians of the forest. That was the end of the great silence. And the world then laughed like clear water as it rushes over the rocks, sang with the sweetness of birds and cried like the wind running through the woods and fields.

But there was no creature on the face of the earth to give thanks for what the Grandparents had done. There were three experiments, but each ended in failure. This was all before the first dawn.

Then the animals showed Ixmucané a mountain, abundant with fruit and corn. She took the kernels of the white corn and the kernels of the yellow corn. She ground them nine times, until the dough was fine and soft. Then gathering the dough in her hands, she created the first four human beings. They were the Maya, the children of Ixmucané.

Introduction

Where the Eyes of the Dead Are Still Watching

The granddaughters of Ixmucané, the women of Guatemala today, live in a land of abundant riches and brilliant colours. But collective grief shapes the soul of the nation. Guatemala is haunted by its unsatisfied dead. As one woman says, "The eyes of the dead are still watching."[2]

Most Guatemalan families have been touched by the mass killings, political assassinations and disappearances characteristic of the past three decades. Unlike Chile, and even El Salvador, there are no political prisoners registered in Guatemala. Anyone who might have qualified is long dead.

Guatemalan women, both *indígenas* and *ladinas*,[3] have been tortured, raped and murdered. They have witnessed the destruction of their families and communities. They have felt the upheaval of an entire society. And they have often been left alone to fight for the survival of their children.

The Maya met the Spanish invasion of Guatemala in 1524 with fierce defiance. Since then, the Guatemalan people have continued to resist their oppressors. In recent years, the women of Guatemala have played an increasingly important role in the struggle for national liberation. Today they are defining the struggle itself.

The Maya

Ancient Mayan society was highly developed and for the most part, patriarchal. Women may have been rulers in Naranjo and Coba,[4] but most women had limited and clearly identified roles, with no access to religious, political or economic power. Most could not own land, or be merchants, priests, teachers or government officials.

The Mayan society reached its height before 900 A.D., building great city-states and ceremonial centres and making important advancements in astronomy and mathematics. The Mayans had an accurate calendar, charted the stars, predicted eclipses of the sun and moon, understood the concept "zero" and employed an intricate written language.

By the time the Spanish invaded, classic Mayan culture was in decline. Mayans had split into several groups, concentrated in what is now Guatemala and parts of southern Mexico, with a sprinkling through Belize, El Salvador and Honduras. The Mayans had also suffered raids by the Toltecs from the north. By the time Columbus reached the islands of the Caribbean, there were three principal groups in the Mayan empire: the Quiché, the Cakchiquel and the Tzutuhil. There were several smaller groups as well.

The Conquest

In 1524 Pedro de Alvarado, a lieutenant in the army of Hernán Cortés, the conqueror of Mexico, led the march on Guatemala. Even Cortés considered Alvarado extreme in his cruelty and viciousness. Alvarado began the war against the Maya with a devastating battle against the Quiché people. Thirty thousand Maya-Quiché warriors fought, and most were killed. "[T]hey made a river of blood...," the Quiché reported.[5]

After battling the Quiché, Alvarado set out against the Cakchiquel. The Cakchiquel recorded their war against the Spanish invaders: "A year and a month had passed since Tunatiċh (Alvarado) scorched the city, when the Spanish arrived in Chij Xot. On the day 1 Caok (March 27, 1527) the great killing by the Spanish began. The people fought...a prolonged war. Death struck us once again, but none of the peoples paid the tribute."[6]

Within a hundred years, some 70 to 90 percent of the Maya were dead.[7] Thousands died in battle or at forced labour. The Maya had no natural immunity to European diseases. Smallpox, influenza, bubonic plague and pneumonia killed thousands more.

Volumes have been published on the effects of the Conquest. But while death by disease, in battle or at forced labour have been given considerable attention, no one recorded the number of Indigenous women raped by the conquerors. Given the tens of thousands of women and men who were killed outright, it is likely that the number of rapes was high.[8] Misogyny and ethnocentrism had already made women an inevitable booty of war in the "old" world well before the time the Spanish mercenaries and adventurers set sail for the "new." For the conquerors, the land was there for the taking and so were women' bodies. Alvarado himself demanded the daughter of a Cakchiquel king as part of his tribute, in an expression of his power over her people.[9]

Colonial Guatemala

During the three hundred years of colonial rule, the remaining Mayan communities were subjected to forced labour and made to abandon their small communities and resettle in seven hundred villages.[10] Displacing the Maya from their traditional lands also made easier their forced conversion to Christianity. The new owners had failed to find the gold or other riches that other conquerors had taken from the Aztec and Inca peoples, but they were eager to build a fortune in agriculture. Where the Maya had farmed for local consumption, the colonists moved into export, first with cacao and then the dyestuffs indigo and cochineal.

Indigenous communities continued to resist the imposition of the conquerors' religion, law and culture. Through a combination of adaptation and rebellion they survived the Conquest and struggled to maintain their cultural identity.

One expression of this resistance is the fine weaving done by Guatemalan women. Spinning and weaving had been a distinctive part of pre-Columbian Mayan culture. When the Spaniards arrived there already were variants in the colours and patterns of the *huipil* and *corte*.[11]

The weavings done today by Indigenous women carry the Mayan past within them:

Despite five hundred years of oppression, the great, logical cosmological and abstract conceptions of our ancestors survive and are carried within our soul like a strong rope... The clothes we wear are an eloquent statement of our historical continuity. It is there we express our cosmological and abstract beliefs, in a plurality of geometric mathematical figures, and in other figures, some complex, apparently unidentifiable, and others simple, but all of them shining within an extraordinary field of colour.[12]

Resistance to colonial rule was not limited to cultural expression or adaptation. There were many uprisings, both before and after Guatemala won independence from Spain. Women played an active part in several of these rebellions. As Juana Vásquez, a member of the Guatemalan Campesino Unity Committee, says, "If there's an uprising, not only the men rise up. The women rise up, everyone together, the whole community."[13] The scattered records of Indigenous uprisings include a few fragments about women's participation.

In 1693, in Tuxtla in the Mexican state of Chiapas, then part of Guatemala, an uprising led to the death of the mayor and his closest advisors. Five women were among the prisoners condemned to death for their participation.[14]

The Rebellion of the Zendals lasted five months in 1712 and was put down only with difficulty. María de la Cruz, of Cancuc, was a leader in the uprising. She claimed to have messages from the Virgin Mary, and her words inspired two thousand "soldiers of the Virgin" to battle the Spanish and the *ladinos*. The rebellion failed and most of the leaders were executed. But María de la Cruz is said to have vanished into the mountains to continue the resistance.[15]

In Tecpán, in 1759, women attacked a contingent of soldiers who were trying to remove prisoners from the town. Seven women, including a pregnant woman, were beaten for being the instigators.[16]

In 1814, seven years before independence from Spain, Francisca Ixcaptá, a forty-year-old woman who could not read or write, a mother of several children and pregnant at the time, led an attack against the officials of her town, Santa Catarina Ixtahuacán. She was arrested but escaped from prison. She returned to lead an attack on the prison. There is no record of what happened to her after the second attack.[17]

Post-Independence

In 1821, Guatemala won independence from Spain. For the most part, the struggle had been between the Spanish monarchy and the Creoles. Any real redistribution of power was not open to discussion. Those who had been pushed to the margin — women, Indigenous peoples and poor *ladinos* — remained there.

Nineteenth-century politics in Guatemala were dominated by the struggle between Liberal and Conservative governments. Elected presidents became dictators, each creating his own fiefdom. When Justo Rufino Barrios donned the presidential sash in 1873, coffee plantations took over the countryside like bad weeds. Vast tracts of Indigenous communal land and church land were expropriated. A new system of debt labour provided the work force for the expanding agricultural export plantations. Poor campesinos borrowed money and then were forced to the *fincas* to work off their debts.[18]

With the land now out of the hands of Indigenous communities and a population desperately searching for work, Guatemala was vulnerable to another invasion, this time from the north. U.S.–based businessmen had been investing in Guatemala since the end of the nineteenth century. The United Fruit Company grew to control the country's ports and railroads and finally its presidents. By the 1930s, United Fruit controlled about 40 percent of the Guatemalan economy.[19]

By the late-nineteenth and early-twentieth centuries, debt servitude would have a special impact on women. In 1887, a new series of regulations were put into place to control *las mujeres de la vida alegre* — "women of the happy life," or prostitutes. Prostitution was legalized, but only in certain brothels. Any woman suspected of "bad conduct" could be picked up off the street and forcibly confined in a venereal disease hospital. She was then often sent to city brothels to work off her hospital bill and any other debts. Many young prostitutes had been domestic servants before entering the "happy life" and had been sexually abused.[20]

The Ten Years of Spring

In 1944, students, professionals and young army officers overthrew President Jorge Ubico and his hand-picked successor, General Federico Ponce Vaides. María Chinchilla, a teacher, was one of several people killed in the uprising.

The overthrow of the generals ushered in the most democratic period Guatemala has ever known, called the Ten Years of Spring by some people and the Revolution by others. The governments of Juan José Arévalo, a teacher elected in 1945, and Jacobo Arbenz, a progressive military officer elected in 1951, encouraged union organizing and set up social programs. Arbenz introduced a cautious land reform program in 1953.

Women won the right to vote in 1945. But unlike the standard for men, only literate women were eligible. Some social programs were aimed at bettering women's position, and several labour laws were introduced to protect the rights of women workers. The first women's organization was formed during the Ten Years of Spring. The group, the Guatemalan Women's Alliance, was supported by María Cristina Villanova, wife of President Arbenz.

Arévalo and Arbenz were decidedly capitalist. Their goal was to make Guatemala a thriving capitalist country, free from its humiliating dependency on the United States. But Arbenz made the critical mistake of expropriating land owned but not used by the United Fruit Company. His administration paid the U.S. giant the amount registered on tax forms, but the company claimed it had been cheated. The expropriation brought the first U.S. intervention in Central America of the post-war era. In part, U.S. intervention would be justified by the Guatemalan government's tolerance of the Communist Party.[21]

In 1954, Colonel Carlos Castillo Armas led a CIA-backed coup. With a handful of men but an abundance of anti-communist propaganda and complementary bombing runs by U.S. aircraft, he delivered to Guatemala a winter which has yet to thaw. A period of violence and death began, comparable only to the Conquest.

Legacy of the Generals

A series of military governments moved to crush all expressions of dissent. Land distributed under Arbenz' land reform was returned to its original owners. The union and grassroots movements all but disappeared. Today the country is still controlled by a wealthy minority, determined to hold onto power by any means. They have relied on both generals and shadowy civilian presidents to administer torture and death. The military, in extraordinary acts of robbery and corruption, have over the years become rich themselves.

In the meantime, life for most people has grown more and more desperate. In work, education and health, women have been the biggest losers. Many women who work for a wage labour on the large agro-export plantations. Agricultural workers now officially earn ten *quetzales* a day.[22] But women workers consistently earn less than men, even when they perform the same tasks.[23]

Women who live in the city have few prospects for a dignified life. Many fend for themselves and their families in squalid, cramped slums. In one squatters' settlement, El Mezquital, 30 percent of the households are headed by women. Guatemalan women marry, on average, at the age of seventeen and have between five to six children in their lifetime.

Women who can, find jobs as domestic workers, where they earn less than fifty dollars a month and are targets of abuse. The sexual abuse of domestic workers is reported to be rampant. Women factory workers endure extremely poor conditions, earn very low wages, face sexual harassment, and suffer discrimination if they are mothers. Conditions are especially poor in the *maquila* factories, where women work long hours in jobs usually related to the international textile industry. These transnational companies are exempt from Guatemalan labour laws and from paying national taxes.

More than half of the women who are economically active — working or looking for waged work — work in the informal sector, selling everything from gum to watermelon slices on the street or in the market. Others earn a few cents selling tortillas or taking in laundry.

Housework may begin at three in the morning and may take up to eighteen hours daily. It often includes collecting firewood, hauling water, washing clothes — almost always by hand in a river or *pila*[24] — preparing food, including the daily husking, boiling and grinding of corn, and the preparation of tortillas, tending animals, gardens and more. One woman, a widow and head of her small family of four, reported making seventy tortillas a day. In addition, the family under a woman's care often includes elderly or sick parents or other relatives.[25]

Almost half of all Guatemalan women do not finish the first year of schooling. Illiteracy rates for women remain high, 61 percent for women nationally and more than 90 percent in some rural areas.[26]

According to statistics published in 1981, the three major causes of death for women aged fifteen to forty-four are intestinal infections, influenza/pneumonia and homicide. The list continues with unattended injury, accidentally or intentionally inflicted, obstetrical causes, heart or lung problems and malnutrition.[27] Nearly one-third of pregnant women are malnourished.

Many women, especially Indigenous women, have also been involuntarily sterilized. Under the cover of the Family Welfare Association (APROFAM), with financing from the U.S. International Development Agency (USAID) and with consultation from the University of Colorado, the Guatemalan government has carried out carefully planned genocide, based on the myth that poverty is the result of a high birthrate. Women have been subject to sterilization at the birth of their children. They have also been injected with a caustic substance to cause permanent scarring of the fallopian tubes. There is no informed consent. Guatemalan women are now known to be one of the populations most affected by campaigns of this type.[28]

Challenging the Generals

Generations of dynamic and courageous leaders have emerged as Guatemalans continue their struggle and broaden it to include the struggle against all forms of domination. As the women's narratives make clear, for thirty years grassroots groups, including peasant organizations, unions, the churches and others have been mounting the most serious challenge for power in Guatemala's history. The final chapter of this book takes up women in the guerrilla movement, a movement which dates back to the 1960s. By the late 1970s the people had risen. Never before had so many Guatemalans been demanding so much.

Military Murderers and Presidential Pirates

The government's response to demands for social justice proved to be more devastating than anyone could have imagined. After the near elimination of the guerrilla movement of the 1960s, the government turned to more selective repression in the early 1970s. Disappearances and individual assassinations became the main weapons against demands for change. In 1978, mass killings began again. On May 29th, government security forces killed more than one hundred

Kekchí peasants in Panzós, Alta Verapaz. Among them was campesina leader Adelina Caal de Makín, better known as Mamá Makín.

One month later, General Romeo Lucas García took power following fraudulent elections. The governments of Lucas García (1978–1982), General Efraín Ríos Montt (1982–1983) and General Humberto Mejía Víctores (1983–1986) stepped up the violence.[29]

After thirty years of violence one hundred thousand people are dead and forty thousand have disappeared. One million people have been uprooted and live as refugees inside their own country. Another 250,000 people have fled to Mexico, the United States, Canada and other countries.[30]

Thinking its job done, the military needed a civilian partner to share responsibility for the deepening economic crisis. Christian Democrat Vinicio Cerezo took office in 1986. He won by a wide majority in elections relatively free fraud. But it soon became apparent Cerezo was not about to attempt to wrest power from the military or the wealthy elite. He told the families of the disappeared to forget the past and gave the military free reign to control "subversion." The military strengthened its control in the countryside through beefed-up "voluntary" civil self-defense patrols, herded rural Guatemalans into "model villages" and "development poles." All aspects of daily life were tightly monitored.

To service the huge foreign debt incurred by the wealthy elite, wages were frozen as the costs of basic goods skyrocketed. Unemployment and underemployment remained a chronic problem.

As Cerezo's regime spiralled quickly downward, rumours of corruption raged and then exploded in his final years in office. It was revealed that Cerezo had been buying islands and yachts and granting himself huge pay increases. In 1991, it was revealed that Cerezo was involved in the international money laundering scandal revolving around the International Credit and Commercial Bank (BCCI). [31]

Presidential piracy aside, the true measure of Guatemala's first civilian government in twenty years is its human rights record. The Mutual Support Group for the Families of the Disappeared reports that during the first four years of Cerezo's five-year term, 4,028 people were assassinated. Another 1,262 were kidnapped or had disappeared. [32]

In January 1991 a new civilian president took office. Jorge Serrano Elías is a member of the right-wing *Movimento de Acción Solidaria* (MAS)[33] party. He is also a former advisor of ex-dictator Ríos Montt. Serrano Elías' first months in power have shown no improvement. It has become clear to most Guatemalans that the country needs more than elections to create democracy.

The Movement Comes Back

In 1985 and 1986 space for political activity opened slightly. Unions and peasant organizations began cautiously to reappear, along with human rights groups and women's groups.

Women organizing in Guatemala face serious challenges. They are living in a society caught in a cycle of violence. Economic, political and military power are profoundly out of balance. Guatemalans at the top of the scale are unmoved by the misery and deaths of thousands. Guatemala is also deeply patriarchal. The subordination of women goes almost unquestioned.

Guatemalan women meet violence in the home, on the street and on the narrow paths winding through the countryside. Violence is the man in Quetzaltenango who murdered his wife when she burned the rice. It is the soldiers who raped eight hundred women in one region, most of them minors, leaving five hundred pregnant.[34] It is the soldiers who slice open the pregnant wombs of Indigenous women.[35] It is the factory boss who beats a pregnant woman. It is the measles, diphtheria, whooping cough, tetanus, polio and starvation that kill children every hour.

Guatemalan women do not want pity. They are coming together to create a new Guatemala over the scattered bones of their sisters and brothers buried in clandestine graves.[36] For the first time, Guatemalan women are challenging Guatemalan men to look at domination on all levels. Guatemalan women and men are engaged in a profound exploration of the relations between rich and poor, Indigenous and non-Indigenous, women and men, humans and the natural world, overdeveloped countries and countries which have been pillaged for five hundred years. The challenge lies in whether popular and revolutionary organizations can transform themselves to include these struggles against all domination.

The revolutionary movement of the 1960s failed in part because most Guatemalans — the people who most desperately needed change — did not feel the revolution was their own. Trapped in the narrow definition of struggle as class struggle only, the leaders of the era did not understand the extent of the oppression and anger of Indigenous peoples. That changed in the 1970s when the massive incorporation of Indigenous peoples transformed the revolution and broadened the field of struggle to include a race analysis.[37] Going beyond class as the sole source of oppression opened the possibility of looking at oppression based on sex.

Resistance to tackling women's oppression has been strong. Lip service has always been granted to women's importance in the struggle, but the inclusion of women's oppression as something fundamental has not been accepted. That is up to now. Since the late 1980s, women have been demanding that their issues be addressed. During one round of talks between the government, the army and the Guatemalan National Revolutionary Unity (URNG), Rosalina Tuyúc and María Teresa Aguilar, two women whose narratives appear in this book, arrived unannounced at the meeting. They came representing widows and refugees and demanded that the talks reflect reality, not abstract ideas.[38]

> The theme of the liberation of women is difficult and profoundly revolutionary. It's difficult because it affects each of us in our family life and in our organized life, and like all revolutionary change, it represents a transformation in the relations between human beings. It means the loss of privileges for some and the accepting of responsibility by others. To oppose the need for this struggle against the patriarchy as something fundamental in our revolution is not to accept the depth of the existing structures of domination and subordination.

> Many of us fear the exploration of (women's oppression) because we have come to realize that the enemy isn't just the soldier, the police, the army, the rich. It manifests itself

in all of us, men and women ... Perhaps it is easier to kill the obvious symbol of our oppression, the beast that destroys our people, than it is to destroy that same expression within ourselves. In reality, it is necessary to do both.[39]

The women of Guatemala have never been silent. They are widows fighting for themselves and for their children, single mothers demanding decent wages for their work in foreign-owned factories. They are teachers, secretaries, tortilla makers, students, professors, housewives and prostitutes. Guatemalan women are in the countryside, in the slums, in the mountains and in the steamy jungles, surrounded by mosquitoes, the shrieks of howler monkeys and the eyes of their ancestors. They are Catholic and Protestant, Indigenous and *ladina*, of European descent and Black. Made by the hands of Ixmucané, the Grandmother, they are the women of Guatemala.

The seed for understanding the structural source of our oppression as women has been planted. But it is like a child that has only just been conceived. We know it is there. We can sense it. It has such a long way to go, changing, transforming, finding its own shape. We are anxious to see this child born NOW! Who will she look like we ask? We would even be happy just to feel the first movements, little kicks, telling us that it is there. We can't rush this process; it will take its time. But this is certain: someday it has to be born. And even now, as we live through these years of violence and lies, its heart is beating.[40]

Endnotes

1. This Mayan creation story is drawn from: Dennis Tedlock, trans., *Popul Vuh: The Mayan Book of the Dawn of Life* (New York: Simon and Schuster, 1985); Adrián Recinos, trans., *El Popul Vuh: Las antiguas historias del Quiché* (San José: Editorial Universitaria Centroamericano, 1987); and from interviews with Guatemalan Indigenous women.
2. Interview, February 1991.
3. *Indígenas* define themselves as belonging to one of Guatemala's twenty-two different Indigenous peoples. *Ladinas* are women whose ancestry is Indigenous and European/Spanish. There are also people of European descent, mostly Spanish or German and there are Garífonas, members of a small Black community in Livingston, Izabal and in the Atlantic port town, Puerto Barrios.
4. William George E. Stuart and Gene S. Stuart Rathje, *The Mysterious Maya* (Washington: National Geographic Society, 1983), p. 73.
5. Cited in Jim Handy, *Gift of the Devil: A History of Guatemala* (Toronto: Between the Lines, 1984), p. 20. The source for Handy's citation is *Titulos de la casa Ixquin-Hebaib*, cited in V. Brickner, *The Indian Christ, the Indian King* (Austin: no publisher given, 1981), p. 40.
6. Adrián Recinos, trans., *Memorial de Sololá: Anales de los Cakchiqueles* (Mexico City: Fondo de Cultura Económica, 1950 and 1980), p. 131.
7. Handy, *Gift of the Devil*, p. 19.

8. Rape continues to be an essential part of the military's counter-insurgency program. The number of women raped in recent years hasn't been documented either. Also, it has been estimated that 50 percent of Central American women refugees fleeing repression and misery in their home countries are raped during the crossing of Mexico. See Tom Barry, *Guatemala: A Country Guide* (Albuquerque: The Inter-Hemisphere Education Resource Centre, 1989), p. 102.

9. Recinos, *Memorial de Sololá*, p. 128.

10. Handy, *Gift of the Devil*, p. 23.

11. *Huipil* and *corte*: traditional dress.

12. Daniel Eduardo Matul Morales, *La ropa que usamos* (San José, Costa Rica: Liga Maya Internacional, 1990), p. 4.

13. Interview, May 1988.

14. Severo Martínez Peláez, *Motines de indios: la violencia colonial en Centroamerica y Chiapas* (Mexico City: Cuadernos de la Casa Presno), p. 63.

15. Ibid., pp. 125–167.

16. Ibid., p. 61.

17. Ibid., p. 62.

18. *Fincas*: plantations.

19. Handy, *Gift of the Devil*, p. 80.

20. See David McCreery, "This Life of Misery and Shame" in *Female Prostitution in Guatemala City 1880–1920* (No publication details available).

21. The Party had been allowed to organize openly. According to Handy, *Gift of the Devil*, pp. 119–121, the Guatemalan Communist Party — later named the Guatemalan Workers' Party — was a minor but honest

political force. There was no question of Party members "imposing" their will; they had to put forward policies accepted by the labour movement's rank and file.

22. One *quetzal* equals twenty-six Canadian cents; 3.83 *quetzales* equals one Canadian dollar.

23. Unless otherwise noted, the information in this section, including statistics on Guatemalan women, are drawn from documents compiled by INE, the Instituto Nacional de Estadistica (The National Statistics Institute) 1989.

24. *Pila*: water trough.

25. Interviews with Guatemalan women.

26. *Situación de la mujer en Guatemala III*, "Mujer y educación" (Mexico City: Publicaciones Especiales 4, Ciencia y tecnología para Guatemala A.C., January 1988), pp. 46–48.

27. *Situación de la mujer en Guatemala II*, "Mujer y salud" (Mexico City: Publicaciones Especiales 3, Ciencia y tecnología para Guatemala A.C., June 1987), p. 24.

28. *Guatemala, A NACLA Report*, Susanne Jonas and David Tobis, eds. (Berkeley: North American Congress on Latin America, 1975), p. 27, describes a procedure used on poor women in Guatemala City, a forerunner to the massive campaign that was to be introduced into the mainly Indigenous Highland regions:

> (A) project which was completed between January and June 1974, consisted of injecting a toxic paraformaldehyde solution into the uterus of women ... The hope is that the solution will cause scars in the fallopian tubes and thereby produce sterility; the idea is that such a method is far easier than the current procedure of tying the fallopian tubes, which requires

surgery. One to two weeks following the uterine injection, the women will have hysterectomies and the removed uteri can then be studied to see if the injection actually blocked the fallopian tubes.

See also, *Situación de la mujer en Guatemala IV*, "Relaciones sociales, políticas y culturales" (Mexico City: Publicaciones Especiales 5, Ciencias y tecnología para Guatemala A.C., September 1989), pp. 27–33.

29. Ríos Montt and Mejía Víctores each came to power through military coups.
30. Luisa Frank and Phillip Wheaton, *Indian Guatemala: Path to Liberation* (Washington: Epica Task Force, 1984), p. 92.
31. Centro exterior de reportes informativos sobre Guatemala CERI-GUA in "Government and Army Officials accused of Coruption," *Monthly Glace*, vol. v, No. 61, Aug.-Sept. 1991, p. 6.
32. *Annual Report on the Human Rights Situation in Guatemala* (Toronto: Inter-Church Committee on Human Rights in Latin America, 1991), p. 11.
33. *Movimento de Acción Solidaria*: Solidarity Action Movement, a right-wing party with international connections to the Conservative Parties of Canada and Great Britain, and the Republican Party in the United States.
34. Marilyn Anderson, *Granddaughters of Corn: Portraits of Guatemalan Women* (Willimantic, Conn.: Curbstone Press, 1988), p. 52.
35. *Guatemala: A Nation of Prisoners* (New York: Americas Watch Committee, 1984), p. 105.
36. *Noticias de Guatemala*, Año 13, Numero 190, julio 1991, Mexico City. In June 1991, Rosalina Tuyúc of

CONAVIGUA made public the discovery of a secret cemetery, containing the remains of one hundred people, beside a school in Chuantlán, El Quiché.

37. Rafael Mondragón, *De indios y cristianos en Guatemala* (Mexico City: Copec/Cecope, 1983), p. 121.
38. *Noticias de Guatemala*, Año 13, Numero 190, julio 1991, Mexico City.
39. Interview with women from the Guatemalan National Revolutionary Unity (URNG), May 1991. The URNG is the united front of the armed opposition.
40. Interview with Marta Gloria Torres, March 1991.

In memory of Adelina Caal de Makín, Mamá Makín —

*A Kekchí elder and leader in northern Alta Verapaz,
Mamá Makín was one of more than one hundred
Kekchí women, men and children gunned down by
the Guatemalan Army in the centre of town in
Panzós on May 29, 1978. She had led a peasants'
movement that demanded title to the land
they worked.*

CHAPTER ONE

Women of the Land

Between half and three-quarters of the Guatemalan population is Indigenous.[1] Most Indigenous peoples live in rural areas, and work the land. Yet nine in ten of farms in the countryside are too small to support families and are becoming increasingly infertile through overwork and dependence on chemical fertilizers.[2] Many Guatemalans today must migrate to large plantations where their wages fall far below what they need to survive.[3]

From cacao in colonial times to broccoli and snow peas today, Guatemalan agriculture has depended on the exploitation of migrant labour. And from the *repartimiento*[4] imposed by the Spaniards to the debt-labour practices brought in with the coffee industry and the vagrancy laws enacted under President Ubico in 1934, Guatemalans at the lower end of the economic scale have created wealth for the elite. At present, no laws force the population to migrate in search of work. The law of hunger is enough.

By the late 1960s, change began to sweep the Guatemalan Highlands. Many Catholic missionaries, inspired by Vatican II, made a conscious "option for the poor" and chose to encourage consciousness raising among poor communities. People began to organize, to study the Bible and then to create cooperatives. At first these were financial cooperatives, and then production and distribution ones followed. Catechists, health promotion workers and literacy workers were trained and projects to improve living conditions were set up. As the pieces began to fit together, the rural population moved into forming campesino committees.

The most damaging Central American earthquake in the twentieth century struck Guatemala on February 4, 1976. It killed more than twenty thousand and left more than a million people homeless. For the most part, only poor people, in their flimsy dwellings, were affected. Relief money and materials flowed into Guatemala and piled up in the backyards of the small ruling elite[5] and the military, bringing to light the extent of government corruption and greed. But in the aftermath of the earthquake communities drew together and strengthened the work of campesino organizations.

But Guatemalans in the countryside soon faced repression. The mass killings at Panzós, in Alta Verapaz, were the first of the late 1970s.[6] Then, on January 31, 1980, a group of twenty-two unarmed peasants, several of them leaders of the Campesino Unity Committee and their supporters, occupied the Spanish Embassy in Guatemala City. Government security forces firebombed the building, killing all but the Spanish ambassador and one campesino, who was kidnapped from his hospital bed the following day and murdered.[7] Thirty-nine people died in total.

The Spanish Embassy Massacre would seem rather minor once the military government of General Lucas García increased the repression in the early 1980s. But it would be the counterinsurgency campaign of his successor, General Ríos Montt, that would devastate the rural population. As he put it,

"We don't have a scorched earth policy, we have a scorched communist policy." The army swept through rural Guatemala, destroying livestock, fields and farms — an entire way of life. Four hundred and forty communities disappeared.[8]

Women were hit hard by the counterinsurgency campaign and then by the continuing military build-up in the countryside. Countless women were raped, tortured and murdered. Countless more were widowed. Officially, the number of widows registered in Guatemala is close to 45,000, but other estimates reach as high as 100,000.[9] The discrepancy is not surprising: a widow is a woman whose husband was "subversive." Most of the people resettled in "model villages"[10] are women and children, as are the refugees in Mexico and the refugees inside Guatemala. And women are primarily responsible for the mental health of their communities and families:

> The problem of machismo is most common among men who have been in the army. Military service is extremely detrimental, divorcing young men from their traditional values... Many return with traits of violence, aggression and attitudes of superiority. After a few years, they gradually assume the values of the community again. Parents and wives suffer greatly in the process. The recovery of these men is due largely to the help and patience of women: mothers and wives.[11]

Despite tight control, rural Guatemalans continue to organize: in the refugee camps, in Communities of the Population in Resistance, very quietly in Guatemala itself, and in the armed opposition. Women, who have always played an important role in campesino organizations, in consciousness-raising groups, as catechists and health promotion workers, are now key organizers in the refugee camps and in the widows' committees.

Despite the government's apparent hope that rural Guatemalans can be held in a state of terror, there are signs that the wall of domination is beginning to crack.

We Value Life Very Deeply:
Five Centuries of Struggle

Juana Vásquez,
Campesino Unity Committee

My name is Juana Vásquez Arcón. I'm forty-three years old, a member of the Quiché people. I'm from the department of El Quiché, from Río Blanco, a community in the country where a beautiful river flows. My great-grandparents lived there, my grandparents lived there. My brothers and sisters and I were born there.

If we were all still alive, there would be eight of us — four women and four men. One of my brothers was killed in the repression and my sister went missing in 1983. We assume she's dead. I have one brother inside Guatemala. The rest of us have had to leave.

My parents were Catholic catechists. My father travelled to several communities to teach the Bible, the catechism, to prepare first communions and weddings. Beginning in the 1940s, he devoted his very active life to Catholic Action.[12] So my mother, sisters, brothers and I were in charge of farming and supporting the family. My mother is from an extremely poor family — they don't have any land. My father's family had a little plot of land; that's what we cultivated.

We start working from the time we can hold a broom or carry a water jug — where we lived in the country we only had one well for everyone. From the time I was very young, I had a little jug for fetching water. We also had to take the animals to pasture. My grandparents had sheep and a few cows, all skinny and shaky, but even if they're skinny you have to take them to pasture.

When I was nine years old, I went to school. I took first and second grade — that was it as far as education went. I would have liked to have gone on with my studies, but the teacher said, "If there are no more grades, you can't." There was a time when the teacher held night-school classes for adults. To learn more, I tried to sneak into the night school. I was eleven. But the teacher told me, "What are you doing here if you've already got your grade two?"

My mother was in the leadership of the women's group of Catholic Action. She had the job of treasurer. I always helped her because she didn't know how to read or write. I kept the accounts, wrote everything — but with her extraordinary memory she didn't miss a thing. She just asked me, "Did you write that down? And that?" She had it all down without a single piece of paper.

We planted corn, beans — that was for us. But we also planted tomatoes and onions to sell. That took a lot of time, it's very hard work. At five o'clock in the morning you have to go to the river to fetch water. We had to go two or three kilometres with a jug on our heads to water the tomatoes. But that was just normal work for us. From the time we were very young, all day, from sunrise to sunset, there we were.

I feel that I lived a campesina's life until I was fourteen. The responsibility of supporting my family is in my blood to this day. I know what a campesina's life is: harvesting beans all day under the hot sun.

But in spite of all this our life was very happy. We needed a little more money for sugar, soap and salt, so we started to sell fruit drinks. I'd be really happy when I earned five cents a day sitting by the highway — that's selling five glasses. All day long with my little jar, all for five cents!

But then we began to go to villages that were farther away. We had to get up at two in the morning to carry all the dishes and other things we needed. Sometimes it was very hard work — it's muddy, or when it's dry it's very slippery. I remember when I almost killed myself under a load — we carry everything on our heads. I fell and everything landed on top of me. I broke all the glasses — at the time we didn't have any money — and I just cried. But my mother said, "Don't worry. The most important thing is that you're alive."

She almost died once beneath a load. She was carrying brown cane sugar — it's hell, it weighs so much. She fell and the basket came down on her chest. She completely lost consciousness.

Now, all that was hard work but I was happy too, to be in the country. I enjoyed taking the animals to pasture, climbing the hills, happy to be in the fresh air. It was a joy to bring in the harvest or to sell my drinks. Really, I wasn't sad during my childhood.

But when I was fourteen I changed a lot. I had always told my parents that I wanted to study more. And they would say yes, they would like their children to have the chance to study. The time came when some nuns came to the village, looking for girls who wanted to study. I wanted to sign up right away. My mother wasn't even at home; she'd gone out selling when the nuns arrived. Only my grandmother was home. "I want to go!" I said. "Be careful. You have to wait," said my grandmother. "But I want to go! I want to go!" I signed up. And when my parents came I told them that I'd signed up and that I wanted to go and study.

It was hardest on my mother because my older sister had married; I'd been her right hand. My other brothers and sisters were still small. I still carried the younger ones. But I convinced them. "Go and try," they said.

I was almost fifteen when I went away to study. I was in my glory. I was delighted with school. Most of us were from Indigenous communities, and they respected our culture. The nuns were very kind and soon we felt close to them. I stayed there for six years, until I was twenty. They gave me the chance to finish my studies, skipping grades. I finished high school the last year.

Then I went to the capital with them, and I entered their convent. I was going to be a nun, and while I was studying to become a nun, I continued my other studies. I graduated with my teacher's degree.

All these changes were very difficult. I suffered from being far away from my community, with only middle-class students. There weren't any Indigenous people there. I had to put on a nun's habit and they cut my hair.

It takes three years to become a nun and three years to be a teacher. I did both at the same time. I felt very out of place. Now I say this, but that was only for a year. At the end of that year I began to like everything. I started changing how I thought about my culture. Now I liked to be in nice surroundings, to have good food, nice things.

It reached the point — and I'm so very ashamed of this, but it's the truth — that I felt embarrassed because of my parents. That was when I was graduating from teacher's college. I didn't want them to come. They were so simple — they were campesinos, and everyone else was going to arrive in suits and ties. I felt bad, and I even told them not to come. I remember once — and now it hurts me so much — I said to my mother "Don't talk to me in Quiché." My mother didn't speak Spanish and I didn't want it known that I was *indígena*. Without realizing it, you get sucked into it and you change. You think you are doing your best, that you're raising up your race, your culture — just because you're studying a bit.

But that didn't last long, thank God. When I graduated as a teacher, I graduated from the convent life, and they sent me back to work as a teacher.

Right away — this was in 1971 — I took a course on Indigenous culture. My God! That's where everything began. I opened my eyes, opened my ears, and I saw my people's reality. I understood what oppression and discrimination are, where they come from. I understood why the poor were so poor. And from then on I began to work, giving classes, working with women in the villages.

I had a chance to travel to many communities. I gave courses on our culture, about our values, about our ancestors. We began to value our old people and to learn from them. I felt as if I had changed from head to foot. I really understood what the Bible says about people saying that the scales fell from their eyes. It was as if I was blind, and then my eyes were opened. Soon our work began to spread through the diocese. I worked in Huehuetenango, Quetzaltenango, Cobán, Sololá, and El Quiché, with all the different peoples. I began to associate not just with Quichés, not just with the people from my village. Now I began to associate with Mams, Cakchiquels, Kekchís, Ixils. I began to have a new vision of the different peoples.

I worked at that for many years. I felt a love for our identity, for our culture. From then on my work has been raising people's awareness. We talked about discrimination, the poverty of our lives, about our values, about our ancestors' values — that it was worthwhile saving them.

I wanted to believe that when we all understood our values we'd rise up and leave our oppression behind. That was our thinking in the early years. We didn't understand that the roots of the problems ran much deeper and that we couldn't bring change overnight. But as we moved forward we began to understand our exploitation — not just oppression or discrimination — and its roots. All this came together from 1971 to 1975.

In 1976 I left the convent. I wanted to devote myself more to the people. In reality, I liked religious life: I received all my education from the nuns, and I had grown very close to the congregation. But now there were certain limitations on consciousness-raising work, so I thought I'd leave for a year. But then the earthquake happened in February of 1976.

It was terrifying in the Highlands. Now it wasn't too bad for us in Río Blanco, but farther south in El Quiché there were thousands and thousands of deaths. I wanted to go immediately to the areas most affected to help with the work. I joined a team in Quetzaltenango.

We went to work burying the dead. It was terrifying. But it made me more aware. Many goods arrived from outside the country to help our people. But the best tents and canned foods stayed in the capital, for the rich in their chalets. In the meantime, poor people lived beneath trees, hiding, with nothing, losing everything. But that helped me. I saw communities helping each other: different peoples, with different *trajes*,[13] different languages.

I stayed with the team in Quetzaltenango. We worked in a town called Zunil. We were there for five years. We held literacy classes, Spanish classes, did consciousness raising. And when I joined the team, we spread the Gospel. Of course, the little nun had to put in spreading the Gospel. We taught the Gospel so people would wake up, so they would come alive.

It was a beautiful experience: reflection, shared living. We began to settle family problems, economic problems. Those who had a little land lent some to those who had none or to those who had no home.

We went to other departments, to other communities. Other groups were forming. We had begun to demand our rights, to demand a raise in wages on the south coast, to hold demonstrations against the high cost of living. Our people began to see that change was possible. We wanted to make a better life. We saw our people suffering poverty, malnutrition, sickness; we wanted immediate solutions. You heard demands from all sides; there were struggles from all directions.

The army didn't like that at all and said we were communists — especially me, Mother Juana. The army came in twice looking for me, in 1979 and 1980. The situation was getting very serious. I left the community; the families stayed. They continued working for a while. By then, it was impossible to communicate with them. Many kept working on their own and were later killed by the army when the repression spread to all parts.

The army doesn't look to see who's who. They sweep through, taking women, children, old people — it doesn't matter. It was horrible to see bodies everywhere. It doesn't matter who you see lying there: he's your brother, she's your sister. To see women torn to pieces, without being able to bury them. You couldn't bury them, first because there were so many, second the army won't let you — they're right behind you. Then, as we fled, we had to go right over the bodies. That's how we got out. How can people do this to other people?

We, the Indigenous people, value life very deeply, not only human life, but plant life, animal life. When I went to take the animals out to pasture, all of a sudden, I'd feel like pulling a branch off a little plant. My grandmother would say, "What are you doing, Juanita? What did that plant ever do to you? It would hurt you if your arm was torn off. It hurts the plant to have a piece torn off it. It's not right. If it's for your firewood, okay. If you're going to build something, okay. But you never tear it up just for something to do."

Respect for life is deep inside us, and after seeing so many bodies, my heart was paralyzed. I wanted to curse the soldiers, but I couldn't find words ugly enough to describe such cruelty. When they really wanted to hurt the parents, they would round up young children and newborns, put them in the house and set it on fire. The children screaming, the mothers crying. What could the parents do? They screamed outside the houses while their children were being consumed by the flames or suffocated by the smoke. Soon everything was ashes. Then came the women's turn.

They rape women in public, in front of their husbands. They swear at the women, make fun of their dignity as women.

You have to ask why. The only conclusion you can come to is that they're giving the soldiers drugs, brutalizing them, making them crazy. They do whatever they feel like. They're crazy. They grab children by the legs and break open their heads against a tree trunk. I saw all this. Sometimes you don't know if a village will be there tomorrow.

In a village between El Quiché and Alta Verapaz people were sleeping peacefully. At five in the morning, soldiers surrounded them. One circle, then another, and then a third — so nobody could escape. They woke people up and brought them together in front of the school and the health centre. First they burned the children. When people saw this, some went running. Other soldiers were ready and rounded them up. Bodies were everywhere. They killed everybody. One man had animals. He got up very early to see to his animals. In a village of two hundred, he was the only survivor — his wife, his children, his parents, his relatives. It was so horrible there are no words to describe it.

We aren't going to forget. And when Lucas García[14] left and Ríos Montt came in — that cruel man was far worse. He said he took power because God gave him the presidency. He was the leader of the fundamentalists.[15] He went so far as to condemn all Indigenous peoples. He went on television, saying that we were dangerous, that we should be killed.

Like our ancestors, we began to defend our land and our lives. They went up in the hills, into caves. That's what we did in 1981. I left the convent permanently. I joined thousands of others. It was something to see: children, newborns, pregnant women, old people, young people hiding under the trees, up in the hills, under rocks, in caves.

We left, taking nothing. I was standing there, with my arms crossed. My only clothes were the ones I had on. It was like that for many people. You eat wild fruit. In the beginning, the fruit was big and ripe. But there were thousands and thousands of us, so it quickly ran out. At first, people went to get corn they'd hidden. But that was running out. That's why we began to plant corn in the mountains. But as soon as the ears formed, the army would come in and cut it down with machetes. It was enough to make you lose all hope.

You feel as if your heart's stopped. But now, in the mountains, you hoped that at least they would leave you in peace. Then they began to send in planes. They'd circle overhead and then nose-dive. "Oh Lord, what's going on?" people would wonder. Then the bombs began to fall.

They dropped bombs carrying a milk-coloured liquid — probably with chemicals to make us sick. People got skin diseases, with pus and boils, blisters that came out under the arms, little bumps. We'd never seen anything like it. They grew bigger and bigger. I had one on my leg. Unless we lanced them with a razor, people died. And then there were ordinary sicknesses too.

But people have held up, despite the bodies, despite the cruelty. On the one hand, it's really been sacrifice and suffering; on the other hand, it's a struggle for life. This sharing between many different peoples from many communities is really something special.

I'd had a chance to study, but to see my people working there — pregnant women there in the mud, giving birth in the bushes — has been the best school in my life. The struggle for survival, seeing that old man, that pregnant woman. Mothers would tell me, "Look at my breasts. I don't have any milk. Nothing to give my child." There they were with cold water and a cloth, feeding their newborn children. That's how women are. You don't see them whining; you don't see them sad, complaining. On the contrary, they're saying, How are we going to work this out? What are we going to do? Somebody gets an idea, and then another thinks of something.

I lost track of my parents for two years. At last, at the end of 1982, I found out where my parents were. My brothers and sisters had gone their separate ways. My sister had been picked up — it's likely that they killed her. My sister Francisca's death still hurts. There was a time — I was crying and crying — I felt as if I'd lost half of myself. We'd worked on the team together. She left three children. Now my only hope is that they can grow up to be supportive and giving, continuing their mother's work in her memory.

My parents are elderly now, but they're always looking for ways to help, wanting to give us energy, to teach us. They never say no, don't go, be careful, something's going to happen.

I spent three years with the Communities of the Population in Resistance (CPR). I left the country in 1984. The Campesino Unity Committee (CUC) broke up because of the repression. We worked in little groups or as individuals. We couldn't continue as an organization, but people who went into the jungle kept on working, those who went into exile kept working, people who stayed in the Patrols[16] kept working. But we were disconnected.

We had several meetings to reshape our organization. On April 15, 1988, we had our tenth anniversary. The government, the army, the rich, wanted to erase the CUC from history. But we're bringing people back together where ties had been cut, and we're organizing in areas where we've never been. We thought it was going to be difficult to move ahead with the struggle. But when speaking to the people inside Guatemala, we heard a different story. Some are afraid, that's normal. We're afraid too, but it's not enough to hold us back.

The CUC has pushed for women. Many of us have become involved at all levels. Women who can't read or write, women who have been able to go to school — all participate in different ways. Women are working in education, in training, speaking at demonstrations, organizing. There isn't one area of our committee made up only of men.

It's been that way from the beginning, because all along consciousness raising was for men and women. As the committee developed, the women developed as well. Some compañeras, the bravest women, can't read or write, but they're analyzing, reflecting; they have positions in the structure. There are some who've had some schooling, but if there is no political clarity, nothing can be done.

The life of a Guatemalan woman who isn't part of an organization is very different and very difficult. Belonging to the CUC means you've broken with the ideas of the past. We've had to shatter ideas, certain conceptions, certain visions of life. For example, before, women belonged only in the kitchen or taking care of the children. If you're not part of an organization, you're at home. You take the animals out to pasture, see to the tomatoes, the onions, go to the market, wash the clothes. That's the old life. But once there's conviction and commitment, these arrangements break down. At times, the man stays behind, taking care of the children; the woman goes to give a talk, to a meeting, to carry out a task in the capital.

Some problems of daily life are the same for Indigenous women, organized or not. If you wear the *traje*, or don't speak Spanish, you can't defend yourself in the markets, on the street, on the bus, at school or at the health centre. You take your child to the doctor: they take care of the others first. And then when your time comes, there's no medicine and they send you away with nothing. When you get on a bus, it's "Move to the back." It's full in the back, and there are empty seats up front. But no, those aren't for you.

They call us "María." María is the campesina María, the Indigenous María, the María who doesn't know anything. When we used to go to the market with our onions and tomatoes, it was "María, how much is that?" "María, how much are these tomatoes?" "Ten." "Five. Give them to me!" They set the price they want.

Then in times of repression it's rape. They pick up their husbands, make their children disappear, rape them, mock them. It's much harder when you're aware because you're clear that it's wrong. It's so clear for you that this is a lack of respect. And the worst is that you can't do anything about it. You have to put up with it or you die.

We're awake now. There is no other way. We've survived five hundred years of cultural oppression and discrimination. The Europeans want to make it into something splendid. They describe it as a meeting between two cultures. Very good; then value our values. We want the anniversary to be an international year in solidarity with the struggle of the Indigenous peoples throughout the Americas, an international year honouring our leaders, who've given their blood for five centuries of oppression and discrimination.

We know we're not going to accomplish change soon. We're coming together, but it's still going to be very costly. We're very clear about that. We want to be active participants in the country's political, social and economic life. We don't want to have just one or two representatives, tokens. We want our entire culture, our entire history, recognized.

Most people in our country are Indigenous. We are distinct peoples, with distinct languages, distinct *trajes*, with particular ways of being, with particular demands. All have the right to carry out their lives as they wish. Our role is to see that our people have their voices heard. We're tired of an elite deciding for the rest of us.

Our new society is going to be something extraordinary and very complex. We can't say there won't be problems, but there's going to be something wonderful, of many colours, like Guatemala.

We Believe Refuge Is a Path with an End

María Teresa Aguilar,
Permanent Commission of
Guatemalan Refugees In Mexico

My name is María Teresa Aguilar. I'm Cakchiquel. I was born in San Juan Sacatepéquez. That's my hometown, but now I live in the Quetzal Edzná settlement camp, in the state of Campeche, Mexico.

Our parents and our grandparents had no land. The only thing they had was the little plot they lived on, so we left our land and went to the south coast, to the plantations to work. They asked for land in exchange for work, or they rented.

When we were grown up — we were seventeen or eighteen — we heard they were giving away plots of land in El Petén, but we were afraid of wild animals. People believed the jungle would swallow them up, that people would disappear. El Petén is very far away, about 400 kilometres from the capital — almost two days away, about a twenty-two-hour trip.

When we got to El Petén, there weren't any large towns — nothing more than small villages, with twenty or thirty little houses. No street, just a dirt road. The land wasn't divided; it was held in common. Then we got organized, thirty-five families; we asked for land from INTA.[17] The land was given to us in 1972, and we began to work, organizing committees to take our demands for schools, health services, roads, clean water, electric lights to the government.

I belonged to the health committee. Before I married, when I was nineteen, a priest sent me to Rafael Landívar University where they gave courses to train community development workers. I learned a little about that, and with the help of other compañeros, we set up committees. We didn't know how to go about it, but you learn by doing.

That's how we got a health station, which was very simple, but we saw it as very important because many women had worked very hard for it.

That was my first experience organizing women. We had fifteen women, including eight younger women. It was very difficult but it was worth it. They gave us medicine and a little bit of help from USAID[18] — a little *incaparina*,[19] oil, wheat and milk. I was head of that committee.

I worked for twelve years as a catechist. I took many courses about life and about the problems that we have. We began to see that we had been blind to our own reality. We used to say it was God's will we were *fregados*.[20] That's not really the truth — it's the will of a few people in power.

That was how the persecution, the disappearances, began. Most of us in Guatemala are poor, and the government began to see that people were organizing everywhere. They began to get written demands. What they call the "counterinsurgency" happened because people were organizing to demand their rights. They saw it as subversive. Then they were afraid.

The government said the *comunidades de base*[21] were responsible for people rebelling. Then they began to take measures against the catechists.

In November 1981, they picked up a man from my community. The death squads took him away in the night, after breaking down his door and raping his wife. On the outskirts of the village, they picked up another man. They took them to the base between La Libertad and Sayaxché, to El Subín. They tortured him, he began to give names. They had a list of names at the base and they began to ask questions. The next day he told where people lived and who they were — as he was dying he gave a lot of names. But really, he only named who he'd seen going to church.

Then selective repression began. They picked up catechists. Later they began to pick up committee heads. Then they picked up those who were organizing cooperatives. It was intimidation, so people wouldn't keep on organizing because that was dangerous for the government.

Then, about six kilometres from where we lived, there was a skirmish between forces from the mountain[22] and the army. They'd taken advantage of a curve in the road and set up an ambush. They caused heavy casualties for the army. They turned a truck over. Some soldiers were killed, others were injured and others went running because the subversives had planted bombs there.

The army came to our community to ask if we knew these people and why hadn't we warned them. We said we didn't know anything, that everyone just went straight home from work. Then the army began to say that we'd helped these people. Everything happened so fast. Nobody knew what was going on.

They said we were providing food for the guerrillas, that we were guerrillas, that we were there during the day but we left at night. People said no, we didn't know who they were.

The army asked us what we thought about the guerrillas, and we answered that we had no land and that the government didn't give us anything. And that's the truth. Then the army said we must be in favour of the guerrillas. Up to that point, people still didn't understand what was happening, but they did have the courage to talk back to the army.

Then, on April 19, 1982, the army set fire to the village. They army came in about eleven at night, in three trucks. One parked at the entrance of the village, and the other two completely surrounded the area where the houses were. They came in, and since the houses were made of palm, they doused them with gasoline and set them on fire.

It was night. Some were sleeping; others were still walking around outside. Then we began to hear people shouting, "Let's get out of here!" Because the night was so dark mothers woke up the smaller children and let the older ones fend for themselves. Others fled in their underclothes. We'd gone to bed sure that nothing would happen — after all we were in our own country. Many people fled without clothes, barefoot. Some could grab their children and leave; others didn't have time for anything and only ashes remained of them and their families.

My family was almost at the end of the village. What helped was that we had a lot planted and we hid there. When they had gone away, we went into the jungle, but they burned our house. Some of the villagers went one way, others went another way. That's how we managed to get out and we hid in the jungle.

The next day the sun came up. We didn't know what to do, we were so frightened. One man said that he was going to see what had happened, see if he could find a little corn or something for the children to eat. So he went into the community. At eleven in the morning, when he went in, the dogs were barking loudly. He was looking for something in the ashes when the army returned.

This man was a witness — he saw how many bodies there were. Some were completely burned, with their children at their sides. He loaded up the tractor and went to a town close by. They had dug a hole with a huge Caterpillar. They buried people on top of each other, about forty-five bodies, children and adults.

Some people went up in the mountains, others to populated areas close by. Others went to other cooperatives. People couldn't get any of their possessions out, not their *cortes*, not their harvest. Nothing. We'd used clay dishes, pots, jugs — the army completely destroyed them. In the dressers, the towels, napkins, were completely burned — everything in ashes.

That's how we left the community. We spent almost two years up in the mountains because we were afraid to go to a populated area due to the list of names. We'd been leaders in the cooperative, others had been leaders of committees, others had been catechists.

That's how people came to seek refuge in Mexico. The first people who came in 1983 lived with Mexicans who gave them shelter in their homes. They gave them corn, clothing, beans. But the police saw this and they called Immigration. Immigration informed the Mexican government. Then the Mexicans got organized. They called the press. The police sent an airplane to bring goods, sugar, beans, rice.

Three days later Immigration came to find out who they were, where they came from, why they'd come, what happened, why people were sick and pale. The Mexican authorities were shocked to see these people and they immediately helped them and told them not to worry. A lot of help came from the churches. They sent clothing, more goods. They lived like that for more than a year — with the church helping with food — while the government organized the Mexican Commission on Aid to Refugees (COMAR), and COMAR and the UNHCR[23] worked out a plan.

In the beginning, people were pretty much all right because they worked. But they weren't paid much. The women had to go and harvest corn or pick chillies so they would give them corn to keep the family going. There was some exploitation of their labour there because they paid them two hundred to five hundred pesos a day. Many women went away to other states. Others left with Mexican women.

The Guatemalan Army was still making raids on this side of the border,[24] and they killed two Guatemalans at the camp in Benemérito in 1983. Afterwards they threw them in the river. At the other camp, Puerto Rico, the Guatemalan Army went in and bombed our fellow refugees.

Then the government[25] felt the Guatemalan Army raids on this side were a problem[26] and that this could cause domestic political problems. And they thought that it could be dangerous for Mexicans who lived near the border. They set up a resettlement plan for 1984, in Campeche.

I have six children myself. And apart from that, I help out seven orphans. Being a mother is a bit problematic. Over time, we've all learned that women are seen only as reproducers — for domestic work, raising children. That's her whole role and nothing else.

My husband understands a lot about the need to work, although there have been times when this has caused difficulties. Sometimes the men aren't very convinced of this. What my husband said to me is that more women have to take part, not just me. Then I said you have to work to get more women, help them understand there's a real need for them to help, to make the struggle theirs too. My children also help. Some of them study in the morning and others in the afternoon. My firstborn is sixteen. They've organized themselves to work in the kitchen and everyone helps me.

In the camp there was a need to organize the women because Guatemala was the site of many massacres and many people left. There are 192 widows and 410 orphans here in the Quetzal Edzná camp alone.

I thought we should come together as women to talk about our problems. It's terrible, everyone isolated in her little house. Who knows if they have eaten, drunk, slept? We began to talk about Guatemala's problems, about what was happening to our brothers and sisters in Guatemala, and about how we all had a duty to talk with our children about what led us to become refugees.

We began to talk with each other, at first to create awareness. Each told her own story — we don't all come from the same department. Next each widow told about how she left, how her husband died. It was a wonderful meeting, and we decided that coming together to talk about our problems as women was really worth the effort. The widows said they cried alone at home, but things needed to be talked about and solutions needed to be looked for.

It's much more difficult for a woman to separate herself from the home. We believe it's necessary to meet together because without our participation, women's voices won't be heard. Only a woman understands the problems the widows have because they have lived them. Only they understand the problems a mother has because they have lived them. It isn't easy to take on responsibilities, but it's necessary to do it.

The president's wife, Raquel Blandón de Cerezo, came in November of 1986 to the camps and said we had to forget about the past. She said there was a democratic civilian government and we could now go back. She said we shouldn't feel resentment anymore, that the past is the past and the present is another reality.

The widows came together and decided what they wanted to say to the president's wife. The women said they felt resentment and they had to show it. Their husbands had died, and their children, and they wanted to talk with her.

The widows dressed in black and they delivered a letter they'd written, saying although they were very grateful they really wanted those responsible for their husbands' deaths and disappearances to be brought to justice and punished.

At the time, people didn't know how to respond. They didn't know what was happening and many of our brothers and sisters were going home. But they weren't being given their land, they were being taken to "model villages."

That's how eight compañeros were named to the Permanent Commission, including two women, although the other compañera is no longer working with us. The community knew about my work record and my experience. They had confidence in me — above all because I can manage Spanish and a dialect. This helps you take on responsibilities. They elected me and I accepted.

We believe we've taken a big step by organizing the Commission. We've managed to get rid of doubts, to say who we are and what we're thinking about in terms of going home. Before they'd say everybody in a refugee camp was a guerrilla and that's why we fled, why we "betrayed" our homeland. But we know we wouldn't have left if we hadn't had to. We didn't understand all this before, but we've come to understand that the problem is that a few people want to keep everything that belongs to all of us.

There are six points that must be agreed upon if we are to go home. They are: the right to land, the right to return to our places of birth, the right to free association, respect for our lives and physical well-being, no army in the areas where we're relocated, the right to freedom of movement.

We know going home is a process — we don't know if it's a medium- or long-term one — that depends on the political will of the Guatemalan government.[27] We see Guatemala going backwards, back to when we left in 1981 and 1982. The death squads, the army, more U.S. advisors, the repression and control of the Indigenous population have increased. They're under tight control and aren't permitted to organize freely. This problem affects all of us.

We know how cruel the army and the government have been. And we believe we have the right to take back our land. Where we are, we're tilling rocks — the land is very infertile. This year we planted three times. And when the corn was quite high, a downpour flooded the cornfields and ruined the crop. We couldn't harvest beans this year because the rains came too soon. The beans were small and now there's a bean shortage.

We don't know when we can go back, but in the meantime, our houses here have turned into colanders. When it rains we have to look for a little corner, all together, until the rain stops.

We're a little sad because we pray for rain and then we ask for it to stop. It's a complex problem. It's so hard being far away from our land — but we women believe refuge is a path with an end.

We Are Not
the Weaker Sex

María Celestina Balán,
The Campesino Committee
of the Highlands

My name is María Celestina Balán. I'm from San Martín Jilotepéquez, in Chimaltenango. Since I was very young I've been concerned about people, wanted to work for the people. I saw their poverty, and I said when I got older I would do something.

I married when I was eighteen. My husband was of the same school of thought. He was Catholic, a catechist. At the time he belonged to a youth group — that's where we met. I told him how I felt, and we decided to go and live in a village far away to see what we could do.

A year later I had my first child. It was difficult, but it didn't stop my need to work. Two years later, my next child came. It got harder for me every day. We kept working; we couldn't stop working just because of that. Soon my other girl arrived — by then there were three — and we kept living in the same place. We'd been working with people there for six years.

Then the situation began to get worse. The government didn't like it much when campesino organizations began to get better organized. We were beginning to think about what we'd call our organization, and we came up with the name Campesino Committee of the Highlands. But nothing happened. This was around 1976 or 1978. We needed a name in order to get some backing, not from the government but from the other communities.

When the repression began to get very bad in 1980, we kept on working quietly, until 1982. Even as the repression continued, we said we had to keep on working, speaking out against what was happening. We couldn't remain silent.

Our area — Chimaltenango, El Quiché, all the Highlands — was hit hardest by the repression. That's where there were the most deaths, the most widows. So there were new needs. There were orphans, widows, displaced people. People could no longer stay where they were; they had to go somewhere else. We had to leave too. In the meantime, I went to live in the city. Later we moved to a different place, but we always had the idea of keeping the Committee going. We thought that this was the only way to be united. Even if we had to walk at night, hungry and cold in the rain, we were prepared for anything but staying where we were. We kept on working, although back then they picked up many of the Committee's leaders. But some of us stayed and we began to work. In 1988 we finally began to come out in the open. We needed to come out in the open not just to make ourselves known nationally, but internationally too.

We can't just sit and cry and wait for things to fall from heaven. We know there are people who want to help, that we aren't alone in the world. There are many people who want to help us. That's why we began to think it was important to leave Guatemala. That's how we began the projects.

As I said, I have three children. As a women it has been very difficult for me. I had to leave my little girl three days after she was born because of the situation. She stayed at my parent's house. Fortunately they were in a position to take the children, so they wouldn't be affected by the repression. I went to get her when she was eight or nine months old and took her somewhere else. It was hard for me and for all the children because they'd gotten used to being with my parents.

I had already had one experience — they had taken my brother away. They didn't find me, so they took my brother. I thought if I left my children, the same thing would happen to them. That would have been too hard for me. What I did was to take them somewhere else. At the time we were without a home, with no safe place for ourselves, let alone for them. Then I began to think about what we were going to do. Because my husband had a lot of friends, we found some who could take our children. That's why we went to the city. It was just for a while.

That was around 1982. I wanted to keep working. I took my children to stay with some other friends who took care of them for two and a half or three years. The only thing I was happy about was knowing that they were alive. They weren't where I would have liked to have had them, but at least I knew they were alive. I saw them for short periods and said I had to keep on working. I could spend very little time with them. At least I had the satisfaction of doing something for our people.

Then, in 1986, when the little one was six years old and the others a little bigger, I began to feel it was necessary to bring the three of them with me. I talked with them and asked them if they wanted to come with me. I told them there was a risk that something could happen to us, but I was going to keep working, many people needed our work. They said I could keep on working, they were going with me. Then the four of us were together. That was a relief. It was as if I could breathe again.

By this time they had kidnapped my husband. He was kidnapped in 1985. That's why I thought it would be better for them to be with me. They knew they had no father, and they said they didn't want to stay alone. They wanted to have someone to depend on.

To this day we don't know what happened to my husband. At one time we still had hope we were going to find him. Later we thought we'd find him, even if he was dead. But we haven't seen him since 1985. It's sad because I'm always waiting to see if he'll appear all of a sudden. But my case isn't the only one. There are many women like me, especially in the Highlands because that's where the repression has been the worst.

For the time being, the Committee plans on continuing the work we've begun, and we hope that the government will let us keep working. But the way we see it, it's possible there will be another repression equal to that of the early eighties. That's precisely why we keep our projects going — because we believe that's the only way we can find a way out of our situation.

The struggle for the land is one of the most important things — we often don't even have a place to plant. We know the land belongs to us, but we often have to rent a little plot of land just to grow food.

Because of the situation we can't go to school. We can't get a diploma, so we can't say, "Let's go look for work." All we can do is go to the plantations, and if you have three or four children you have to take them along. You go to the plantations and if you get work they set down a whole bunch of conditions. They tell you that you're going to work from six to six, for the pay that they decide on, not what you really should earn. You don't know if you'll come home with all your children. Many times we've seen women leave with five children and come back with one or two. The rest have died of malnutrition or sickness. Children can't stand it on the coast because of the climate and the poor food. They get diarrhea and they die. If it's not that, then the children get poisoned by the spraying.

Women are without husbands, without any help from anyone, and then on top of that, their children die. There are times when they're left alone, completely alone, without any hope. They hit us from one side and then the other because we're women. They've said we're the weaker sex, that we are ignorant. And in the end we suffer doubly. We are not the weaker sex; on the contrary, there are many examples of women who have carried on in spite of the situation.

What has happened is that the system has forced this situation on us because it doesn't want women to develop themselves. I believe that men and women have the same rights. The truth is that as well as being mothers, we can work. We can if our husbands or compañeros help us.

If I'm not here someday, I will have gone with the security that I participated in the struggle. I'll be happy because of that. Many women have given their lives. That's why I have confidence that it will change some day, that it won't always be as difficult as it is now.

We've Really Been Able to Resist Everything

Paula Carmelita,
Communities of the Population
in Resistance

My name is Paula Carmelita. I am an Indigenous woman from the Jacalteca group. My birthplace is Jacaltenango, in Huehuetenango. There are nine children in my family, seven sisters and two younger brothers.

My parents lived in Jacaltenango. Then they heard that two priests had bought land in Ixcán, in northern El Quiché, and were dividing it up for different families. They brought us here to the Ixcán in 1972. I remember I was six years old. We had good land, and little by little things began to develop. People from different ethnic groups, from different towns came here — Kanjobals, Mams, Cakchiquels, Quichés, *ladinos*. Villages began to develop, and we began to plant cardamom, coffee and other crops. And then the harvest began to come in. But there were very few years we lived here in peace.

Then, all of a sudden, the repression began in the 1970s. In Ixcán, we'd set up five villages. The army came into each village and set up its bases. We trusted them. We thought they were there for us, for our well-being, to take care of us. But all of a sudden they began to kidnap people. One morning a man had vanished. Or they took away another man's son, and so on. Little by little, the situation got worse. When we saw how it was going we thought we'd better leave, go to our little plot of land. In the village we had a little house, nothing else. When the army saw people were leaving their homes, they burned down the base and went away. We were happy. The army was gone, now there would be peace.

Then they hit us hard. In Cuarto Pueblo, one of the villages, they slaughtered 378 people, including women, children and old people. That was Sunday, March 14, 1981. People didn't know what was going on. Some were shopping in the market; others were worshipping in church. The army came in and burned all these people. I lived in Mayalán; Cuarto Pueblo was on the other side.

I was at home with my family when we saw smoke was rising. And then, gun shots. That day — I remember it was about five in the afternoon — we fled up the mountain. The army came to the house and there weren't any people. They found only animals and all our belongings. We didn't take anything with us, just one or two bundles of clothes, whatever we could get out. What was left behind was left behind. So the army came in and they burned everything. They killed all the animals. Not just at my house, but of all the families there. There were twenty families in this area alone. We went into the mountains together, into the jungle to hide from the army.

The first days were very difficult. It rained a lot, and we were all used to living in houses. We weren't prepared. We had no experience; we didn't know how to live. There were so many children. My little brother, he was eight months old. He was just learning to crawl, and I remember my brother beginning to walk, in the mud there in the mountains. And not just him, many other children too.

Many people arrived without blankets, without clothes; they'd left with nothing. We came together, huddled like groups of little animals. We didn't know what to do. Later the army came deeper into the mountains, and many families were found and killed. Women would just be crossing a fallen tree with their children when the army would shoot and kill them. In 1982 sixteen families were picked up. Many of them were killed. We were hit very hard, without knowing how to defend ourselves.

There's a lot of suffering. We had to make huts out of leaves — we couldn't cut down trees because the army would hear the noise. That's how we build houses when we don't have any metal or plastic roofing. In the beginning, the women cooked at night. We couldn't cook during the day. We couldn't build a fire — we couldn't let the smoke rise because the helicopters would see it. Women had to get up at two in the morning, and put out the fire at five-thirty. No fire all day, and the food that we'd made the night before was frozen solid. A child couldn't cry loudly; you had to cover its mouth. If a rooster crowed, you had to tie its beak. It was hard. We're used to shouting and laughing, to talking and singing. We couldn't even take a walk in the mountains. So many died. They couldn't stand so much dampness, so much mud. When the children began to cry — into a cave, so the noise wouldn't get out.

Another difficult thing for women is when they give birth. That's the most difficult. There were always midwives in the community before and we all left together. They pretty much knew how to take care of the women. But there's never any medicine. There are a lot of little plants they know how to brew as a drink or for a compress. But sometimes the army is right on top of an area where these plants are and we can't go in. What happens is there are so many people that we always have pregnant women. Sometimes the situation is normal when it comes time for the birth. We can take care of her, give her a warm drink. But many compañeras give birth during bombings, under machine-gun fire, when the army's coming after us. Then it's just: get the baby and go!

In 1983 people began to ask: what are we going to do? There are so many of us. We wanted to live together. But we couldn't, so we divided into groups to make everything easier. Then we would sleep together, but we went our own ways to work. One day the men are coming back from work. One doesn't show up, then two. The army has picked them up. This made us work collectively. We sleep together, we eat together, we work together. That's when we set up our security so the army couldn't pick us up as easily.

That's how we began to come back to life in 1983. Our supplies were running out. The clothes, boots — almost gone. No crops. Nowhere to earn money. That's when people set up the Ixcán Community Committee — seven compañeros with the authority to watch over the community's needs. Then we set up local committees, with two catechists, two health promotion workers and one literacy worker for every group.

By 1984 we had a little experience. By 1985 we were more or less used to this way of life. We'd learned new things. We began to look for great big tree trunks, to burn them in the night, and then we'd have hot embers all day. Then we could heat tortillas or a drink, and eat warm food.

By 1987 some communities had been in the same place for five months. Other communities have lasted for up to a year. And it isn't that the army hasn't come looking for people — they know that people are there, but we've learned how to protect ourselves, playing cat and mouse. When the army comes we're on the move. Sometimes we've been in a place only half an hour when the army comes and we have to move. Sometimes we've just put our bags down.

The hardest thing for a woman is to be with her children. If the army comes in all of sudden — and there are two or three children — she has to take the children, she has to carry the suitcase, she has to take the food, a thousand things. The time comes when the compañeras tell their husbands, "Don't go to work, because we can't get the children out. What? What's your problem? You just take your machete and go off to the fields. If the army comes, you take off running. How am I supposed to run?"

We've suffered, but we've also learned to solve our problems. And something we women have learned to do is stand up for our rights and be proud. It's something new and it is a little hard to do. Before women felt that because we couldn't read or write, we were only good for the kitchen, to take care of the children and all that. But now in the Communities in Resistance, we've seen a change in ourselves. Now many women are literacy workers, health promotion workers or catechists. Some young women who didn't want to be health workers or teachers, they wanted to work with a machete, so they went to work with the men.

These are the young women. Mothers with children five or six years old don't want to go very far away, so they organize the gardening. We have gotten hold of cabbage, tomato, lettuce, carrot and radish seeds. The mothers go out at six in the morning and come back at ten, because they can't take the sun. They work fast and come back.

The most beautiful thing has been that we've learned to work collectively. We're clear that not only men can do things. Women can too. We all work together: men, women, children and old people. The old people can't carry a load, but they can cut corn. We all participate; now we don't just rely on the men.

We're called the Civilian Population in Resistance because we've really been able to resist everything they've thrown at us: bombings, machine-gunnings, destruction of our crops. Everything. Our Lord has given us the spirit and strength to resist. It's not that we like this situation, with airplanes overhead. But if we leave, if we abandon our home, who is going to look after it? We're here to defend our land and the land that belongs to the refugees. We hope that someday they'll come back and be with us.

We know it won't always be like this, dark all the time.

We're always explaining to the children. There are a lot of children who were five or so when they came to the mountains. So they remember their homes and they talk with the smaller children. The children are always asking questions. If the smaller children are cutting down a tree, the fifteen- or sixteen-year-olds tell them, "Don't cut down the tree. That's our house. It's because of the trees that the army doesn't finish us off."

My little brother — the one who learned to walk in the mountains — is seven years old now. Sometimes he asks, "Why are we living like this, Mamá?" When we go to the fields it's sunny, but his eyes can't take the sun. Then we begin to talk about why we're here: "It isn't because the mountain is our home: here's what happened…"

I Wake Up Early in the Morning, Expecting to See Him at the Door

Ana Isabel

My name is Ana Isabel. I'm from San Juan Comalapa, Chimaltenango, and I have three children. I'm a widow — my husband was kidnapped, and to this day we don't know whether he's dead or alive.

He's a peasant. I don't think he was mixed up in anything political — he was never a member of any group or anything. He came home to eat, and we went to the fields together. Maybe it was out of jealousy... I don't know.

This happened in 1981, on September 20th. We were asleep. These heavily armed men came in, about eleven at night, and they said they only wanted to talk with him. They needed to talk to him alone. I asked them why they were taking him. If they wanted to talk, they could talk in the house. But they said it had to be just him and for me to keep quiet and not do anything. If I did, they were going to kill my husband right there at the door.

It was because I was afraid they were going to kill him that I let them take him. I was holding onto him. They pulled my hands away, and they put their weapons to my chest. They told me to keep quiet: they only wanted to ask some questions and he would come home. I haven't seen him since. He left me with two children and at the time I was expecting another. I was two months pregnant and my little girl doesn't know her papa.

I'm always thinking about him and I wonder. I hear there are a lot of refugees in other countries and it makes me think maybe they took him far away. But I don't know. I've never gotten a note or anything. If he was alive, maybe he'd send me a note or something written; but I think they killed him.

I'm always sad. I have three children, and right now, it's hard, even if you work and work. I'm a woman who weaves, who works and everything, but my earnings are never enough.

When they kidnapped my husband we had a little plot of land and I kept working it. But it's very hard because of the fertilizer. Now even if I look for a hired man to help me work it, it's not the same. My husband was the owner and he knew how to work it. I couldn't make ends meet; I was paying more than I was taking in. That's when I decided to come here.

The nuns had put up an announcement in the church, but I didn't pay much attention to it. It wasn't until later, when I felt I couldn't go on any longer, that I began to think about the children's studies. My work doesn't bring in enough. I worked weaving with a loom and by hand. I like to keep my children clean and all that takes money.

Now I've been here for three years, taking care of the children, making their food, washing them, teaching them whatever I can. And because my children are here, I've liked it. I make food for all the children, including my own. Right now there are twenty-six children and three women — although there are days when we have errands to do and one of us has to stay alone. So I've taken care of the children by myself and that's hard.

There are around twenty-two women in this project, some of them widows, others young women. Each has different problems. Some have had problems with an alcoholic husband or they've been deserted. Many were widowed by the violence. It's hard here in Guatemala. They don't stop to see if you're guilty or not; they just find you and take you away. Sometimes they'd go out in the country and those poor people would never make it home. Usually they wouldn't check to see if they'd been involved in something or not; they just took them away as if nothing mattered, even children who hadn't done anything. A child doesn't know anything. At least we understand what we get involved in and why, but not the children.

About twenty other women were widowed the same night I was. A lot of people left the village after that. Before that I'd told my husband we should go to Guatemala City. I'd grown up in the capital, I was born there. My parents are from Comalapa, but they went to the capital to look for work. When my mother died I went back to my village with my grandmother. So I pretty much knew what the capital was like and I told him we should go. I thought it would be quieter there. But he said, "What about our land? I'm not guilty of anything. They won't come for me. Don't worry. God will protect us." So that was that.

Now the situation is calmer, but at the time you couldn't do anything. Even if you heard somebody being killed, you didn't go out to see who it was. You were too afraid. And anyway, if you went out, they'd kill you too. Everything is a little calmer in my village now, but you still hear about what goes on. Three nights ago they say they killed seven men in Patzicía, a village close to here. They took them away and killed them, like they did my husband.

I never found out who did it. You can't see them: they wear masks, big hats and high boots, and they're heavily armed. They were tall men. My heart says it was the *judiciales*,[28] but I'm not sure. The guerrillas just killed those mixed up with the army; they didn't kill civilians. But the others, they came in cars and grabbed anybody. Even the National Police have committed many crimes.

My children — the first is ten, the second is eight and the youngest is seven. I hope for the best for them, but money talks. If you don't have money, you can't give them anything. What I want to do is to teach them how to weave so they can work and, with God's help, earn a living. While I'm still alive I'm going to do whatever I can to give them the best. Fortunately, they're happy here. Sometimes they remember our family back home and sometimes they think if they had a father maybe they'd be at home. Then I tell them we have to accept it. I tell them he had a fever. It's too hard for me to tell them what really happened; maybe when they're older I'll tell them.

Even though I haven't told them the truth, they're always talking with their friends. One day the youngest asked me, "Why did they take my papa?" I couldn't answer her because I don't even know why they took him away.

Most of the children here are orphans or without their fathers or mothers. There must be thousands and thousands of orphaned children in Guatemala. This has deeply affected the children — some of the ones here saw them kill their parents, their brothers and sisters, their grandparents. So they've been left without any family or anything. In this house alone, there are four children who say they saw them kill their mama. I don't know what to say to them. So I tell them they killed my mama too, so they won't feel so sad. Or I tickle them so they forget. It affects even those of us who are older. After hearing so many stories...

So many Guatemalans are in other countries. I don't know

if they were kidnapped, or if they got frightened and went to other countries because of all that's happened. At least this helps me a little. It gives me hope. I wouldn't know what to do if he came in the door one of these nights. If he's been alive all this time, what's he been doing? Maybe I'd be frightened. Or happy. Or maybe I'd get mad about seeing him after so many years. Maybe it would be better to know he really is dead. Instead, there are times I wake up early in the morning, expecting to see him at the door, and I get frightened.

Endnotes

1. Frank and Wheaton, *Indian Guatemala*, p. 10.
2. Ibid., p. 39. See also James Painter, *Guatemala: False Hope, False Freedom* (London: Catholic Institute for International Relations, 1987), p. 9.
3. According to a 1980 report of the U.S. Chamber of Commerce on its members in Guatemala, none of the U.S.–based transnational corporations it contacted there said it was "experiencing or expecting to experience any unmanageable labour problems." "Political agitation," the report said, "is imported rather than internal." Cited in Tom Barry and Deb Preusch, *The Central America Fact Book* (New York: Grove Press, 1986), p. 23.
4. *Repartimiento*: an "assessment" forcing up to a quarter of the people of a village to work for landowners. Proclaimed under the New Laws of 1541, the system operated until the end of the eighteenth century. See Handy, *Gift of the Devil*, pp. 21–23.

5. Traditionally, the mainstay of Guatemala's small ruling
    elite has been in the agro-export sector of the economy.
    But now it includes wealthy families from other sectors.
    According to a report prepared for the U.S. International
    Development Agency (USAID), "This is a very small
    group with very extensive influence in all areas of
    public and economic life — a group that must be led
    not pushed." Instituto de Ciencias Ambientales (ICATA),
    "Perfil Ambiental de la República de Guatemala," April
    1984. Cited in Barry and Preusch, *Central America Fact
    Book*, p. 225.

6. In the mid-seventies, oil deposits were discovered in
    Alta Verapaz. Once known as the Northern Transversal,
    the area came to be called the Zone of Generals.
    General Lucas García's family became one of the
    largest landowners in the area, with a one-hundred-
    thousand-acre ranch. Kekchí campesinos who had tradi-
    tionally worked the land in zone demanded legal title.
    They were told the land question would be settled. On
    May 29, 1978, several hundred campesinos met in the
    town centre of Panzos. Soldiers opened fire on the
    crowd, killing more than one hundred men, women and
    children. Their bodies were buried in a mass grave dug
    two days earlier. See also Barry and Preusch, *Central
    America Fact Book*, p. 233.

7. The Spanish Embassy Massacre took place in
    downtown Guatemala City, and film footage of it was
    broadcast on national television. Four women died in
    the firebombing. The Spanish government recalled its
    ambassador and severed diplomatic ties with Guatemala.
    Although the Campesino Unity Committee lost many of

its top leaders in the attack, it organized a massive strike of sugarcane and cotton workers two weeks later on the coast.

8. Painter, *Guatemala: False Hope, False Freedom*, p. xiv.
9. *Situación de la mujer en Guatemala IV*, p. 18.
10. In a move reminiscent of Vietnam, Indigenous peoples fleeing the scorched earth campaign were herded into "model villages" as part of the government's pacification policy.
11. Comite Pro Justicia y Paz de Guatemala, *Life and Values in a World of Oppression* (city of publication unknown: Comite Pro Justicia y Paz de Guatemala, 1990), p. 4.
12. Church-sponsored Catholic Action was set up to head off reform and to attack Indigenous spirituality. It was only later that Catholic Action became linked with struggles for social justice.
13. *Trajes*: mode of dress.
14. President of Guatemala from 1978 to 1982.
15. Right-wing Protestant fundamentalist groups.
16. Civil Patrol duty refers to the "voluntary" twelve- to twenty-four-hour shift required of all Indigenous men between the ages of fifteen and sixty, to be performed weekly or once every two weeks without pay. Anyone unable to serve has to pay a fine or pay someone else to take his turn. Any man refusing to participate is labelled a "subversive." The Civil Patrols are also a human shield for the army during its sweeps in the countryside. At the height of conscription, more than one million men were participating. See Handy, *Gift of the Devil*,

pp. 262–263, and Barry and Preusch, *Central America Fact Book*, pp. 235–237.

17. INTA: the National Institute for Land Reform.
18. USAID: the United States Agency for International Development.
19. *Incaparina*: a cheap high-protein flour made of cotton-seed, sorghum, corn, yeast, etc., used to prevent protein-deficiency diseases.
20. *Fregados*: screwed around with, messed over, hard done by.
21. *Communidades de base*: grassroots groups associated with the Catholic Church and committed to social justice.
22. Guerrillas.
23. UNHCR: United Nations High Commission on Refugees.
24. Into Mexico.
25. The Mexican government.
26. Raids are still going on. In June 1991, the Guatemalan Army crossed the border into Mexico, along the Usumacinta River. Civilians living in the El Petén area were forced to flee, losing all their belongings. Twelve people are reported to have been killed in the raid. (CADIP, the Support Committee for the Internally Displaced People of El Petén, in a letter dated June 4, 1991.)
27. The Mexican government is putting pressure on Guatemalan refugees, giving them until 1992 to return or become Mexican citizens. In June of 1991, the Guatemalan government broke off talks with the Permanent Commission, refusing to discuss the six conditions Aguilar outlined and accusing them of having

connections with the URNG. *Permanent Commission Press Release in Centro Regional de Información Ecuménica CRIE #274* June 18, 1991, Mexico, pp. 8–10.

28. *Judiciales*: paramilitary forces with ties to the Guatemalan military.

In memory of Sister Victoria de la Roca —

A member of the Sisters of Bethlehem, Sister Victoria de la Roca was kidnapped on January 6, 1982. Forty-four years old and terminally ill with cancer, she was tortured and shot.

CHAPTER TWO

Christian Women
Take a Stand

Traditionally, the missionary's Bible accompanied the *conquistador*'s sword. During the Conquest, Indigenous peoples were ordered to submit to the rule of God and the Spanish Crown or be crushed.[1] The Church continued to enjoy considerable influence over Guatemalan society until 1871 and the beginning of Liberal rule. Liberal policy wrenched vast tracts of land away from the Church.

The Church retreated, but crept slowly back into Guatemalan daily life during the first half of this century. It helped to topple progressive President Jacobo Arbenz in 1954.[2] But following the coup, many members of the new Catholic religious communities were non-Guatemalans, without ties to either the government or the elite.

In the 1960s, Vatican II and the Medellin Conference of Bishops encouraged nuns and priests to take up social action. This "preferential option for the poor" set loose a conflict within the Latin American Church that continues to this day. The traditional hierarchy remained committed to the established social order and backed the authorities, while priests and nuns living in villages began to set up cooperatives, Bible study groups and peasant leagues. Some became committed to the fledgling revolutionary movement of the sixties and were expelled from the country.

By the mid-1980s, a large number of nuns, priests and church workers, Catholic and Protestant, had been kidnapped or killed. The diocese of El Quiché was shut down after an attempt on the bishop's life. Again, some religious workers joined the armed resistance. Others fled the country, some later forming the Guatemalan Church in Exile.

In the 1980s, right-wing Protestant fundamentalist sects advanced on Guatemala.[3] The more traditional Protestant churches have been in Guatemala since the latter part of the nineteenth century. But newer, U.S.–sponsored sects have made the most headway in recent years. Preaching the gospel of personal salvation and actively discouraging social action, these sects flourished during the dictatorship of born-again-Christian General Efraín Ríos Montt, who declared his presidency a gift from God.[4]

In the meantime, others in both the Catholic and Protestant churches continue their commitment to the poor. In 1983 conservative Archbishop Casariegos, famed for having blessed army vehicles, died. He was replaced by the more progressive Próspero Penados del Barrio. The 1988 Bishops' Conference released a strongly worded pastoral letter, "The Cry for Land," on Guatemala's urgent need for land reform. In 1990, Guatemalan churches united in the campaign Working Days for Life and Peace. The churches have also been key in negotiations between the guerrillas, the government, the army and other groups in Guatemalan society. Bishop Quezada Toruño, head of the National Reconciliation Commission, serves as mediator in this delicate process.

Both the Mutual Support Group for the Families of the

Disappeared and the Guatemalan Widows' National Coordinating Group sprang from the Christian community. Both groups later broke direct ties to the Church, whose support had been cautious and limited.

Guatemala is a deeply religious country. Any movement hoping to transform it must take into account both Mayan and Christian spirituality. Women, while still excluded from the Church hierarchy, are among the chief builders of the grassroots Church. Women remain their children's first teachers of religious and moral values. As the following narratives reveal, these values sustain the struggle and the commitment to seeing it through to the next stage: the reclaiming of power by the people.

I'm a Woman Who Has
Touched Reality, Then Books

Julia Esquivel

I remember a few images from my childhood. One is a photograph in an old album of my father's: he's very young, prostrate on the ground in a street in Quetzaltenango. He'd been shot for taking part in overthrowing one of Guatemala's worst tyrants, Estrada Cabrera, who held power for twenty-two years.

Another impression is of him sitting in front of his huge cabinet radio, listening faithfully to news about the Second World War. I came up to him and I heard those strange names: Mussolini, Hitler. And I began to ask questions: What is war? Why do they kill?

I remember a lawyer who'd been a political prisoner would visit us. He was extremely pale and later I found out about the use of torture. I was finishing primary school during the demonstrations against Ubico and the fall of Ponce Vaides in June and October of 1944. The principal would invite people to come and talk with us. One man came and talked about the situation of poor children who had no shoes, beds, lunch, school, books. Their only right was to work from an early age and sleep on newspapers on the sidewalk.

My own conversion was something else. I hadn't been a Christian from early childhood or been given a religious education at home, but one Good Friday, when I was just barely seven years old, I heard the story of the Crucifixion. That Easter I found my faith. What touched me was the physical suffering of Jesus on the Cross. I wanted to follow Jesus, not so much for my own salvation, but His suffering on the Cross awakened compassion in me. Of course, my understanding was very limited, but I think God accepts and understands a child's heart more than we think.

Those were my first impressions. I finished secondary school and worked as a teacher in the school where I'd studied. I began to study education. But later, in 1953, I went to study at the Latin American Biblical Seminary in Costa Rica. It wasn't just for one denomination; people from all churches went there. And this helped me because it broadened my horizons. I was sitting, eating, studying and celebrating the Lord with Anglicans, Baptists, Methodists, Free Brethren, Lutherans, everyone. Ecumenism was very rare in the fifties.

I decided to continue studying, to finish the ministry course. I decided at that time I wasn't going to get married because I began to feel life with a person who preached but who used a way with words, an ability to convince, for a certain kind of mission wouldn't be the life for me. This was very, very hard, almost an existential crisis. It didn't have to do only with my relationship with one person, it had to do with something more profound — a style of religion.

When I finished I returned to Guatemala and I knew I'd become a stranger because of the environment I'd been in. I'd been in contact with other churches and Guatemala was very sectarian. I was marked, and marginalized from the ministry. There was a time when I wanted to be a minister, to have the legitimacy of the church, to work with the people in the interior of the country. I dreamed about this, but later it was very clear this would be impossible for me.

I sought work at the Latin American Evangelical Institute, a secondary school. I worked there for twelve years. Then, in the sixties, a friend and I went to the City of Children, a detention centre for youth, and asked the principal if we could teach a Bible class.

The first time I tried to talk with the kids, it took only ten minutes for me to realize that it was going to be impossible to carry out our plans the way we'd thought. These children were from desperately poor families; many had fathers who had deserted the home. It wasn't unusual for the mother to have three children, each by a different man. They were deeply wounded by poverty: they didn't have shoes; they didn't get enough to eat; they were forced by their mother, father or stepfather to work, selling newspapers, shining shoes, cleaning cars, working in the markets or stealing. They saw their mother in the morning, after she had spent the night working as a prostitute. There are many cases of homosexual prostitution and incest, sometimes to earn a few cents, or so the older people won't hit them. The girls suffer sexual abuse by their uncles, their stepfathers, their neighbours.

It's very complex, and when you go and talk about the love of God to these children, it sounds so false, so theoretical, so rhetorical, and it is. Little by little, I became convinced that these children were the logical consequence of the abnormal situation in Guatemala, a situation so unbalanced — economically, socially and culturally — that most Guatemalans don't have regular meals, schools, enough clothes to live with dignity. I'm not a sociologist — I'm a woman who has touched reality, then books. The way a country treats its children and adolescents is a measure of how humane or inhumane the society is.

That was my second conversion. When I heard these young people tell their stories, they were like sermons. In their voices I heard a cry for help. What does it mean that the Kingdom of

Heaven is for children? The Kingdom of Heaven means compassion, drying the tears of the weeping, giving rest to the weary, bringing justice to the hungry.

Then I reflected on this: perhaps I am too emotional? It forced me to reflect deeply on what it means to be a Christian. It forced me to take literally the words of Jesus: "For your fruits you shall be known, not for your words, nor your preaching, nor your songs, nor your doctrine..." Today there are many churches that say that you only need to be concerned about the spiritual. Surely Jesus wouldn't have been able to enter these churches. Jesus was concerned with the people. When the multitude was following Him, He didn't tell His disciples to have a prayer service. He told them: "Feed the people," and He gave them bread and fish.

These children, these adolescents brought the Gospel to me. They questioned how far my faith in Jesus went. Was it a faith only concerned with personal salvation, leaving aside those who suffered? An egotistical faith? A faith that only went as far as my interests? It wasn't easy.

I had a chance to go to a place close to Geneva for nine months to take an ecumenical course in theology, with people from more than sixty countries participating. Living and sharing with people from Africa, Korea, Russia, Greece, Egypt, Ireland, England, Australia broadened my horizons more than the course itself. There are as many ways of living the Gospel as there are peoples and cultures: God isn't Guatemalan and doesn't belong to any specific church.

I returned to Guatemala and began to work with an organization called the Evangelical Assembly for Social and Cultural Service. The magazine *Dialogo* was born in November 1970; we also had radio programs on different stations for ten or fifteen minutes, where we tried to speak to Christians about our responsibility to share what God has given us. We began to visit Protestant and Catholic churches. We were sent to work in San Pedro Ayampúc where we began a small project in support of the ministry of the priest at San Pedro. He had fourteen villages; it was too much work for one man. We set up a pediatric clinic for Indigenous children and their mothers. We also had agricultural training and literacy programs.

I visited a development project in Huehuetenango, co-operatives in Ixcán, Jocotán, Cobán. I went to the peaks of San Marcos, visiting San José Ojetenám, Tajumulco, Las Cruces, Ixchiguán — places where people were wasting away from tuberculosis. I've known the campesino movement from the beginning.

I went to the Ixcán in 1975, after the army had kidnapped some cooperative leaders. I had a chance to speak with campesinos who'd been tortured, and with widows. We published their testimonies in our magazine. So I began to have problems early in 1976. A journalist warned me that the G2, the military police, were looking for me. But then the earthquake came and I guess they forgot about me for a while.

One day when I was on my way home an army truck was parked right on the street near my house. A man got out — he must have been in the military — and he insulted me very aggressively. At the time, it was as if I'd gotten a shock. I said, "Sir, you're right. Take the keys and back my car up. I can't do it." And I put the keys in his hands. He was a little bewildered by this and he got in the car. He backed up, farther and farther and farther. He got to the corner and got out. Then I turned around and went to some friends' house for help. My name was on the army's list.

It wasn't the first time. But this time I was very, very, very frightened. When I thought about it, I began to see what could happen in the future. I escaped, and after going around the entire city, I went to the coast. I went on a trip to Santa Lucía Cotzumalguapa. I'd gone there almost barefoot because I was really in a bad state.

I went into the Church of Our Lord of Compassion and I did all the Stations of the Cross. I would have liked to have been alone in the church, to speak out loud because the Stations of the Cross were my people's Stations of the Cross. When I finished there was a Virgin and I went to speak with Her. I said, "You understand me." And because I couldn't do anything else — I couldn't throw myself on the ground and say "Here I am!" — I took my national identification papers and put them in the alms box. That was my surrender. If anyone had seen me they would have thought I was crazy.

Asleep in Santa Lucía, I had a nightmare. I woke up screaming "Where is Father Rutilio Grande?" They'd just killed him. After I woke up screaming I went out in the street, and Father Walter Voordeckers came out to tell me to go back to the parish house. When I turned around to look at him I saw the face of death, and I didn't want him coming close to me. And when I looked at what I thought was the main church in Santa Lucía, I saw it in ruins. Perhaps I saw that because of what was to come later. Walter's death,[5] the disappearance of Conrado de la Cruz,[6] the departure of the bishop.

I saw everything in ruins. Then I went for a walk and I saw a golden circle coming towards me from far away on the horizon. It came closer and closer until I asked it not to come any closer. Then I heard it say, "There will be a new dawn."

In that vision of terrible agony and terror, God was always

with me. After about a month, it ended. It ended in Santiago Atitlan. I went there with some Indigenous friends for three or four days, sleeping, sleeping, sleeping because I was exhausted. They woke me up to eat fish. On Palm Sunday, I had a beautiful vision of the Eucharist. The men had gone down to the coast to cut *pataxte*,[7] and sweet-smelling fruits. When they arrived in the Highlands the fruits were ripe, and then they drank *cusha*[8] and smoked tobacco and danced. It was a symbol of communion, of happiness. But not because there had been a solution.

Afterwards I had a depression that lasted about eight months because I was afraid of the vision. I was afraid of how complicated human beings are, and I didn't feel strong enough to live through what I knew was coming. I could feel it, and I knew that it was going to be very hard. In reality, it was much worse than I'd imagined ... the genocide of my people.

We want peace in Central America but not the peace of the graveyard. We don't want war. We want a peace founded on respect for the lives of children, for Indigenous women, for workers, for campesinos, for the earth. I think about those women whose husbands were assassinated, women who've been raped who knows how many times. This hasn't been going on for just a few years: this crucifixion dates back to 1954, and earlier. The most recent war has been going on for thirty-five years, but for centuries a small group in power has closed its eyes to humanity, to the dignity of the majority. There are women in villages in El Quiché, in Chimaltenango, in Escuintla — who knows how many places? — whose names we don't know, who are determined to put an end to this someday. It's a miracle.

It's been beautiful to have visited so many corners of our

country, so many paths, so many villages. There are many experiences, faces, *trajes*, words I keep with me. This has enabled me to live outside of Guatemala, knowing that these people are there and that they are struggling.

Mary Was Not
a Silent Woman

Sister Eugenia

Now that the whole world is preparing to celebrate the five-hundredth anniversary of the Gospel coming to Latin America, it's more important than ever to remember our history. It shouldn't be a celebration but rather a commemoration of the coming of the Spanish to the Americas — where we can regain the few benefits religion brought.

As Christians, we're all in agreement there wasn't any real spreading of the Gospel during the time of the Spanish. We know what they called "Christianity" was an imposed religion. It forced Indigenous peoples to accept a God they didn't know — a God who, according to the Spanish, had so loved people He sent His Son to die for us. That was the theory, but in practice it meant total slavery for Indigenous peoples.

I believe Indigenous cultures have, over time, made Catholicism their own and have interpreted it in their own way. Now, thank God, they've made it into a force for liberation.

Our people are religious, whether it's the religion of their ancestors or Christianity. As well, we have to value and to make use of everything that encourages the true spreading of the Gospel. Catholicism has to be a liberating religion. If it isn't liberating, it stops being Christian because Christ is the liberator from all injustice. And this is how the Church began to change.

This began in the sixties, with the celebration of Vatican II, and more specifically in the seventies, when the Guatemalan Church began to be more committed to the people and to change. The Church has always helped the poor, but the change came when the Church accepted a commitment to be with the poor, running the same risks the poor must run.

In 1970 I went to work in the north of Guatemala, in small villages where there were often no schools, no drug dispensaries, where children died of hunger and malnutrition, without even the water to prevent dehydration. That's when you begin to feel powerless under this unjust and immoral system.

In one village a measles epidemic broke out that could have been prevented with a vaccine. That month sixty children died in the village and we couldn't do anything. Just call for help, for doctors to come, for clean water and a sewage system. Nobody came to help. Coffins went by, day after day, with the children who'd died in an epidemic that could have been prevented so easily by government action.

It's not necessary to be a great thinker to see this extreme injustice. You only need to open your heart. You don't have to study Marxism or anything. Our people live with injustice. We began to see that God wouldn't want this immoral situation: if we're all children of God, He must be an unjust God to bless some with everything and others with nothing. It's simply an immoral structure — a structure set up throughout Latin America to oppress the majority while the few have more than they need.

It's often said that the Church does "great things" to increase people's awareness, but I believe it's the opposite. These "great things" we were doing were just literacy programs, health care programs — mostly preventive health care. We had programs for the women: sewing, weaving,

Spanish and, in some cases, a few consciousness-raising sessions.

But often when we thought we were increasing awareness, the people were much more aware than we were. Perhaps what we did was to bring a new Gospel, something that wasn't imposed. On the contrary, there was constant reflection on what the Lord is telling us in the Bible. First they taught us and then we took up the Gospel together.

Liberation theology is the Word of God made truth in Latin America: a theology that comes from the poor, born of the oppression Latin America endures, born of our reality. It's seeing the injustice, hearing the cry of the people. It's: What is God's word on this? As Christians, how do we confront poverty and oppression?

The first step was to become aware of reality, but we couldn't just stop there. If as a Church we had kept silent, we would have been cowards, going completely against the Gospel. Jesus bore His people's suffering. But then He spoke out about the situation. So we took the second step, speaking out about injustice. But how were we to act?

We needed to understand where poverty comes from. There are three explanations for it. The first, the least genuine, is the belief that people are poor because they are stupid. For years the Church's answer was paternalism: we must give to the poor. It saw the poor individual, but not poverty.

The second explanation comes from developmentalist theory: poverty is a collective phenomenon but the cause is underdevelopment. They say: we're going to develop and therefore end poverty. So often people are given tools to try to organize themselves, but the roots of the problem remain untouched.

The third explanation of poverty views it collectively and structurally: there can be no solution unless there is an alternative, a different society where there is structural change. When you understand oppression, you opt for change: it can't be solved by good works or through development. It's the only path to the Kingdom — a true Kingdom of God on earth, where there is community, where the values of the Gospel are truly lived.

The Bible inspires me, the words of the Virgin Mary when she finds herself with Elizabeth, and she bursts forth with a marvellous song, The Magnificat[9]: "My heart praises the Lord ... for He has remembered His lowly servant.... He has stretched out his mighty arm and scattered the proud with all their plans. He has brought down mighty kings from their throne and lifted up the lowly. He has filled the hungry with good things and sent the rich away with empty hands."

These words from the Bible, words spoken by a woman, are an inspiration to me. Mary is often interpreted as a silent woman, but she felt her people's aspiration for liberation and could express it beautifully in song.

The time comes when you must speak out; otherwise you stop being a Christian. So we began to work for change. That was our terrible sin. Working for change means you become "subversive"; you become a "communist" because you've understood the real cause of the problem. This resulted in many of us being accused of being "subversives."

Leaving Guatemala was very difficult for me. But the campesinos told me, "Look, Mother, nobody else can go and talk about what's going on here." This was in 1981. And it's true, a member of a religious order has more credibility in many situations.

Bishops in many countries have forgotten their people. But in Guatemala at least some bishops are with the people, through everything. You see this in pastoral letters, in sermons and often even in their very silence. But they are there. At the same time, nuns and priests are still working with refugees inside Guatemala. The strength of the Church lies in our catechists. There are catechists throughout Guatemala who are bringing the Word of God, despite the many problems and risks. And the lives of nuns in Guatemala have been exemplary. In areas where priests have been removed from their communities, or kidnapped or assassinated, nuns have taken up the work of priests, spreading the Gospel.

When we're outside the country it's often the women who speak with the voice of the Guatemalan people. Many in religious orders are working in solidarity with our people. Indisputably, women are going to have to be part of all aspects of building a new society and of the Church. When the new society is established women will have a much greater role to play.

Women have always been discriminated against in our society and in the Church too. As women within the Catholic Church, we're always speaking out against discrimination. The Catholic Church is much more masculine than feminine — women are marginalized within the structures of the Church. But thanks be to God, women aren't marginalized within the liberation of the people. On the contrary, women have played many important roles within it.

Women in the Church will have to play a new role, one we are already taking up. This role will be much stronger in a society where we all have the same rights.

We are a people who have suffered so much, a people with

great courage. Many have died to preserve their dignity. Dignity will be the fruit of a just society, where we all can see each other as brothers and sisters, where Indigenous peoples have full rights, where women can participate fully.

The Kingdom of God must be here on earth, and Christians who understand Christianity are ready to build it. Hope can't be separated from faith. On the contrary, they go together.

I'm with My People

Mother Francisca

I've lived the religious life for more than twenty-two years, in El Quiché and Huehuetenango. Most of that time I've worked in El Quiché, at two different times. The first ended on July 19, 1980, when all religious orders left El Quiché because the army was killing catechists, priests and preparing an ambush for the bishop. So we went to the capital, Guatemala City, to see how we could keep on working.

No one in the capital even knew this was going on. They were killing catechists in Nebáj, Uspantán, Chicamán. Landowners in those areas were paying people poorly, and when workers began to demand fair wages and their rights, the army said the guerrillas had infiltrated. The army didn't stop to see who were guerrillas and who weren't. The plantation bosses were Protestants, Pentecostals, and they said the priests were responsible. Thousands of catechists died. The Church spoke out against the massacres; then the ambushes, the kidnappings began. There was a lot of persecution against religious orders.

We didn't want to leave. But we took it as prophecy and left to make El Quiché's problems known. We thought if all religious orders left El Quiché, we could make a significant statement. A lot of people didn't understand. They said we left because we were afraid.

The catechists were left alone. One priest returned, Father Juan Alonso. Earlier they had killed Father Faustino and Father Jose María. When Father Juan Alonso went back, they jailed him, tortured him and shot him. He had to walk around wounded until he died. The situation was very serious. But one thing must be clear: we never, never abandoned our people.

Slowly, members of religious orders began to return to El Quiché. First four priests, and then in 1985, some religious communities came back. In 1986, members of Roman Catholic religious communities were serving in the schools, the work that we do to this day. We haven't been able to open the parochial school, but we give special classes in the public schools. We're doing other work too. We are fixing up the house, selling used clothes to buy paint. In 1985, we began to give the sacrament again, and we began to train catechists and to assist the community.

In 1987 we began to go out with catechists to outlying communities. Everything was very subdued following the repression. We began in small villages, cautiously, measuring our words. The situation is still very delicate.

One important project we began in 1985 was with widows and orphans. We give classes for the children and set up different projects with the women: sewing, weaving and natural fertilizers. There are two hundred widows just in the town of Santa Cruz. The most serious problem they have is housing. We've bought land and are building houses for twenty widows. They are helping in the construction, so they'll feel the houses really belong to them.

There's the problem of the fundamentalists forcing their way into the country. The sects took advantage of the situation when there were no Catholic religious orders in El Quiché. "Come with us. Denounce the guerrilla catechist." The army even gave special cards to Protestants.

A good example of the difference between the two groups is that once a large group of people came down from the mountains. They'd been running for years, without health care or good food. People were dying of hunger, dirty and half-naked. The children were crying and everyone was afraid. The army allowed us to go in, and a group from the sects went too. We began taking them food. In the meantime, the group from the other church took out their little accordion and began to shout and sing, "Hallelujah! Hallelujah! Praise the Lord that these people have returned to the world."

I have faith in God that someday we will leave this horror. In the meantime, I'm with my people.

Endnotes

1. Handy, *Gift of the Devil*, p. 21.
2. The U.S.–based United Fruit Company was the chief target of the Arbenz government's land reform, introduced in 1952. Under Operation Success, a CIA operation approved by then–U.S. President Eisenhower backed Colonel Carlos Castillo Armas in a successful coup against Arbenz. CIA Director Allan Dulles and his brother, U.S. Secretary of State John Foster Dulles, had been members of the New York law firm representing United Fruit.
3. Traditionally, the Central American country with the highest rate of Protestant churchgoers, Guatemala is now about one-third Protestant. See Tom Barry, *Guatemala: A Country Guide* (Albuquerque: The Inter-Hemisphere Education Resource Centre, 1989), p. 81.
4. General Efraín Ríos Montt is an elder in the Protestant evangelical, fundamentalist church El Verbo. Current president Jorge Serrano Elias is also a member of El Verbo. Ríos Montt received financial, political and

moral support from the New Right in the United States. One strong backer was the Christian Broadcasting Network of Virginia, a network known for its antagonism towards the women's movement anywhere.

5. Father Walter Voordeckers, a Belgian priest serving the parish of Santa Lucía Cotzumalguapa, Escuintla, was killed May 12, 1980.

6. Father Conrado de la Cruz, a Filipino priest, disappeared May 1, 1980.

7. *Pataxte*: a fruit that can be eaten or the seeds of which can be ground and used for a beverage, like cacao.

8. *Cusha*: a fermented drink made from the maguey plant.

9. English version taken from *Today's English Version*, Luke 1: 46–49, 51–53.

In memory of Rosario Godoy de Cuevas —

A founder and principal organizer of the Mutual Support Group of the Families of the Disappeared (GAM), twenty-four-year-old Rosario Godoy de Cuevas was found dead in a ravine with her younger brother and young son in April 1985.

CHAPTER THREE

Women in Human Rights Organizations

Most of the members of Guatemalan human rights groups are women. Women seeking the whereabouts of loved ones, or teaching the constitution to poor campesinos, are threatened, abused, raped, kidnapped and murdered. In 1966, twenty-eight labour leaders and members of the Communist Party were rounded up. They vanished. The Spanish noun *desaparecido* took on new meaning. More than forty thousand people are missing in Guatemala, making it the leading country in Latin America for disappearances.

From the beginning, family members have come together to demand the return of their loved ones. Guatemalan actor Doña Juana Loza de Molina was one of the first to try to organize the families of missing persons. Her son, student Juan Luis Molina Loza, disappeared in the late sixties. Doña Juana demonstrated in front of the National Palace demanding his release. The security forces nicknamed her "the crazy woman." Eventually, she was abducted and committed to a psychiatric institution. She was released only after a doctor, an acquaintance of her son, recognized her.[1]

The Committee of the Relatives of the Disappeared and the

National Human Rights Commission were created in the 1970s. Both shut down after their leaders went missing or were killed. Irma Flaquer, a well-known Guatemalan journalist and founder of the Commission, was kidnapped on October 16, 1980.

In June 1984, a small group of women came together in the Mutual Support Group for the Families of the Disappeared (GAM). The women had met each other in morgues and hospitals as they searched for their vanished husbands and sons. In the beginning, the women hoped their loved ones would be returned to them. They organized meetings and masses and met with President General Mejía Víctores. On October 12, 1984, they set out on a nineteen-kilometre march to publicize their demands. One thousand people took part, the first open demonstration of protest in Guatemala since May 1, 1980.

GAM staged events that attracted national and international attention. They had more meetings with the president. They directly accused the security forces of kidnapping their family members. In turn, the government openly threatened GAM to disband, "or else."

On March 30, 1985, GAM member Héctor Gómez was kidnapped, tortured and murdered. Five days later, Rosario Godoy de Cuevas, her twenty-one-year-old brother and her two-year-old son were found dead in a car at the bottom of a ravine in what appeared to be a faked accident. Reports were that Rosario had been raped and her baby's fingernails ripped out.

On April 13th, GAM held a defiant march. More than one thousand people turned out: "At least two-thirds of the GAM participants were poor peasants, most of them women. Some had gone without eating to pay for bus fare to the city, after having heard about the march on the radio."[2]

The Centre for the Investigation, Study and Promotion of Human Rights (CIEPRODH), formed in 1987, collects, documents and publicizes human rights abuses. As well, refugees inside Guatemala have come together in the National Council of the Displaced People of Guatemala (CONDEG). In 1988, members of the Civil Patrols who wanted to disband their units joined forces. Set up by President Ríos Montt in 1982, the Civil Patrol program conscripted all men from rural Guatemala between the ages of fifteen and sixty. By day and by night, patrollers walked the streets of their villages and towns, forced to monitor population movement and report anything out of the ordinary to the military.

The Civil Patrols have created considerable hardship for an already over-burdened rural population. In July 1988, the Runujel Junam Council of Ethnic Communities (CERJ) brought together close to six thousand campesinos in the Highlands. Their goal is the disbanding of the Civil Patrols. Their work is based on Article 34 of the Guatemalan Constitution of 1985: "The right to freedom of association is hereby recognized. No individual shall be forced to associate with or form part of self-defense groups or associations or similar organizations."

The Civil Patrols have had special consequences for women. It has been reported that in several parts of the country women have been forced to patrol, either in place of their husbands, or sons, or because they are widows. Women have also suffered sexual abuse by the military, while their male family members have been out on patrol. Generally for women, civil patrols have meant a breakdown in family and community structures, resulting in, among other things, increased domestic violence:

Before the army and the so-called civil self-defense patrols came, my husband and I shared all our ideas and dreams. Now everything's changed. Now he doesn't share anything with me, and when he talks to me he yells. He always asks me who I talk with and what the people are saying. He doesn't tell me anything when he comes back from an "emergency mission." He's always depressed. The children are afraid of him because he hits them, even if they just ask him something. Yesterday my mother told me that it was my husband that denounced our neighbour Tomás Macnac because he didn't want to patrol. They found Tomás' body on the side of the road with his hands cut off. I don't know my husband anymore'[3]

CERJ, CIEPRODH, CONDEG and GAM continue, despite daily threats and acts of violence. In 1990, Guatemala earned the shameful distinction of being the country where the highest number of human rights monitors were killed.[4]

We Aren't Widows

María Isabel Choxóm López,
Mutual Support Group (GAM)

My name is María Isabel Choxóm López. I'm originally from the western Highlands, from Totonicapán. That's in the Quiché cultural area. My background is purely Indigenous. But the pressure for assimilation was so strong we completely lost our customs.

I'm a rural primary school teacher and a social worker. That's why I'm here in Tierra Nueva II. I'm not a founding member of GAM, but I'm on the board of directors. GAM was born June 5, 1984. I joined about a month later, when the group was already publicly known.

I joined GAM because my compañero, Gustavo Adolfo Castañón Fuentes, was kidnapped on May 24, 1984. He was a student at the University of San Carlos. My husband wasn't alone — he was kidnapped with two other compañeros. It's not easy to talk about this. You lose someone you loved, someone you've shared with. What I've tried to do is just keep going — to get over it. But I can't completely get over it. We had so little time together; we'd lived together for just a month. Whether he's dead or alive, I can't forget and I don't want to. The consequences have been very, very serious. I felt utterly alone.

With some members of my husband's family, I began a personal search. Looking back, joining GAM helped me a lot emotionally and spiritually because I could channel my hope, my faith and my struggle.

When I joined GAM there were already seventy to one hundred families involved. The kidnappings in Guatemala didn't begin in 1984 — that started many years ago. Then, when the group went public, people looking for an alternative way to search for family members began to join.

I remember perfectly that, back then in 1984, we hoped our family members would appear alive. We made the rounds of the jails, we went to the courts, we asked for interviews with government officials. At the time they were responsible to General Mejía Víctores.

As the year came to an end, we began to realize it wasn't going to be easy to find our family members alive. This led to changes, not in our objectives but in our demands, particularly in 1985, after the assassinations of two compañeros, Héctor Gómez Calito and Rosario Godoy de Cuevas. With their deaths we realized it was very unlikely we'd find our family members alive.

At that time we demanded the establishment of an investigative committee to clear up the whereabouts of our loved ones. We knew who the responsible parties were, but we didn't say anything because we didn't want to hamper any chance they would be returned to us alive. But with the murders of our two compañeros we realized what GAM was facing. Later we suggested the category "political prisoner" be created — it's not humane, but it isn't as inhumane as "disappearances." But it was all turned down.

We continued to fight for an investigative committee. One of the most important events was when President Cerezo[5] took power. We'd talked to him during the occupation of the Cathedral, at the end of October 1985, a few days before the elections. We had the idea he could make a moral commitment to the families, and once he was president, we could demand he keep that commitment.

In effect, he promised to help us. But once he was in power everything was different. In the end, we had a series of interviews with Cerezo, but his response was that we should accept declarations of death, something we flatly rejected. There were a series of manoeuvres aimed at confusing the wives of men who are missing — for example, declaring them widows and the children orphans. This is something we won't accept. We aren't widows and the children aren't orphans. We aren't widows until they prove our husbands are dead. At the same time, we're demanding trials and punishment for the parties responsible.

In 1988 our field of action became broader. We weren't only speaking out about the disappearances: we were also demanding an end to the "self-defense patrols,"[6] protesting assassinations, mass killings and the violations of workers' rights. The beginning of the investigation into clandestine cemeteries was something very important: it's become a source of information for investigating the disappearances.

To date, we've found four clandestine cemeteries, with about twenty-five bodies.[7] They've all been identified. All were killed by the armed forces or by patrol leaders. Three trials have begun, but they're moving very slowly because there's no interest in seeing justice done.

Now we're looking at different problems: for example, at people who are persecuted, people who are having to seek refugee status in other countries because they've committed themselves to the struggle for human rights and for labour and economic rights. But I want to emphasize that we haven't lost sight of our fundamental objectives: an investigative committee and the trials and punishment of the parties responsible.

We're opposed to amnesty. We are never going to accept

amnesty — it would be an insult. It's offensive; it's one more violation of the right to life and liberty.

We've received a lot of offers from President Cerezo, but we've never gotten any concrete answers. Action is what's brought results. Our experience shows this is our only path. So we carry on with our demonstrations, our blockades, our constant protest.

We estimate about forty thousand people have disappeared here in Guatemala from 1966 to the present. It's incredible. Sometimes it's even inconceivable: we simply don't know where thousands and thousands of people are. We really don't know; we can't even begin to imagine what has happened to them.

I'm a social worker. After I joined GAM, I committed myself to the group for the whole of 1985. I wasn't working. I'd had to leave my job. It was very difficult for me to find work because we were well-known, and they'd already begun to accuse us of being "communists," "subversives," "guerrillas."

I knew a priest, a very good friend. He was working here in Tierra Nueva II. All this community had was an attempt at a school, not even a real school. He offered me work here as a teacher.

Later, we began to talk with other compañeros and the priest about setting up a project here. People have been living here for three years; there are almost seven hundred families, including displaced people — people who've come here to the capital, refugees. The makeup is very complex and the community lacks all basic services. There's no water, no electricity. No transportation until a year ago, and then only after a lot of difficulties. No health centre, no school. Nothing from the state. Now there's a school, but it's part of our project. There's a daycare centre, a medical clinic, a small community pharmacy and a literacy project. But all this is totally independent of the government.

We're trying to do things so we won't just be providing assistance, although that's very difficult because the needs here are so extreme. We're trying to make it so that people from the community are in charge of the projects, but it's a little bit of a challenge.

There's no security here. People are squatters and that's illegal — people are ready for eviction at any time. They keep them in doubt, never telling them whether they're going to give them the land. And besides that, INSIVUMEH, the geological institute, has already declared the land uninhabitable: it's completely surrounded by cliffs; it has four gorges, and there could easily be a landslide, destroying the community. But people insist on staying; they have nowhere else to go. That's why we're working here. This is our third year working here, and we're very satisfied because, despite the limitations, it's direct service for the community.

The group working here is made up of fourteen men and women. The daycare centre has been of direct benefit to mothers. In general, mothers who work here in the centre have the greatest needs: they've been abandoned by their husbands, or their husbands are alcoholics, or irresponsible.

I'm very interested in women's issues. Maybe here, and in GAM itself, is where we see the enormity of the injustices towards women. But we must focus on them from the structural point of view, not as the primary problem. We have oppression, injustice, repression, insecurity, and this affects the entire population. But, within these same economic, political, social, cultural structures, the most directly victimized are women and children.

If you go to one of our demonstrations, you'll notice that most of us are women. And we're women who have discovered our capacity for struggle, our capacity for resistance. We've been left alone with four, five, six children, and we have to keep going. It gives me great hope.

Those theories that women are weak or whatever can be overcome. But it won't be easy. We aren't in favour of a struggle between the sexes. Women and men have to come together to forge a new society, and within this new society, we each have to struggle for our place. Only our concrete efforts will achieve this.

Every Time I Went Out
I Was Followed by
Unidentified Men

Mercedes Gómez

My husband's brother had disappeared, so while I didn't participate directly, I was involved in some joint work with GAM.

My husband was involved with GAM from the very beginning, in 1984. Back then it was so small there was no board of directors. No permanent meeting place either. But soon they got more organized and began to make leaflets and everything. I remember when he came home with a banner for the first time. They were going to have their first demonstration. After that more and more people began to come to meetings, people with relatives who'd disappeared.

My husband went to speak with President Mejía Víctores. Around that time, the group began to work more in the open. And that's when the problems began. He'd been getting death threats almost from the beginning. In 1985 it got worse. I didn't know anything about the death threats, not until after they killed him. I guess he didn't want to scare me. I do remember he told me twice that maybe we should start to save some money, in case we had to leave the country. Sometimes telegrams would come; he would look worried, but he'd tell me he felt bad because things weren't going that well with GAM. Once he told me that when he left a meeting he saw a car of *judiciales*, but he thought they were there to watch Nineth or Rosario. I had a feeling something bad was going to happen.

The day before they killed him, I was going to go to

Antigua, about four hours from Amatitlán. He'd told me he was going to buy a chicken on his way home, so I wouldn't have to cook anything. I know he didn't want to go to the meeting that day, but he said he had to go: they were organizing a big demonstration for April 13th. I'd made tamales to sell, and he told me not to worry, he'd be back in time to sell them, if I hadn't gotten back from Antigua. When I got back I thought he'd be there, but he wasn't. I thought it was very strange — it was past five in the afternoon. But I thought he'd stayed for a mass GAM was having that evening, so I didn't worry too much.

At around nine-thirty, when he still hadn't come, I went to tell his family, and we called Nineth and Isabel to ask about him. They told us that he'd left about three that afternoon. We went everywhere — even to the police and to the home of a man in GAM who lives in Amatitlán. He told us they'd left the meeting together, but that he'd gone to buy chicken. That night I didn't sleep at all, waiting for him to open the door.

In the morning, I went to my in-laws to wait for news. Around ten in the morning, a man came on a motorcycle, saying there was a dead body on the road. About ten minutes later, a friend of my husband's came and said for sure it was him, dumped at the side of the road, and that it didn't look like an accident. I couldn't believe it. To think that the day before he had been talking with me and now he was dead. It was very hard for me.

I went home and Nineth and Isabel came over. They asked if he'd turned up. I said yes, but he was dead. They said they'd seen a disturbance on the highway and thought it probably had to do with a dead body. They never imagined it could have been him. A woman living in front of where they'd dumped him said she saw the body there at four in the morning, but she thought it was a drunk. Later, someone else told us he'd seen the body there when he'd gone by on the last bus, at nine-thirty, so we think they must have killed him the same day. He was in terrible shape when we saw him. They'd pulled his teeth out with pliers and cut out his tongue. He didn't have too many bruises — just on his chest which was purple and black, like they'd hit him with a heavy club. On his forehead, he had a big dent. It looked like they'd hit him with the butt of a rifle, like the ones the police use. That's what smashed his skull. The autopsy said he died from injuries to his liver. He also had his back all terribly scratched, as if they'd tied his feet and dragged him behind a car.

Three days after the burial, they came and burned his grave, all the roses and the banner we'd put on his tombstone. We went to see and it looked like they'd tried to open his grave.

It was the army. There's no doubt about it. The same Mejía Víctores who'd told a group of journalists that if GAM didn't stop getting involved, he was going to take "more serious measures." A few days later, they killed Rosario. The day of the funeral there were *judiciales* everywhere. From then on, I accused the government of being directly responsible. A journalist asked me if I wasn't afraid to say that. I told him it was the truth — if they killed me it would only prove my accusations. At first I really was afraid.

The night they killed him I was waiting for him, outside on the sidewalk with one of my neighbours. A car from the local police kept passing back and forth in front of us, until my neighbour said we'd better go inside. They already knew that he had been killed. Afterwards, they used to drive up and down in front of the house, just to intimidate me.

My children had gone to Antigua with my mother that day and didn't return until the next day. It was hardest on my oldest son, who was eleven at the time. He saw what they had done to him. My middle girl was eight years old. The youngest was only two years old. He kept saying he'd seen his papa in the park, and he'd told him he loved him very much. Even now, he sometimes tells me he's seen his papa or talked to him. They were very sad and frightened, didn't want to go to school anymore. I didn't want to go out either: every time I went out I was followed by unidentified men. That went on for three months after his death.

Finally, we decided to leave the country. We applied at the Canadian Embassy,[8] and we were accepted as refugees. Almost immediately we came to Canada. We were very scared when we came; we didn't know the government was going to help us. I thought we were all going to have to work, even my children. We felt very afraid and alone at the airport and at the hotel.[9] But people started to come to help us and everything began to get better.

It was hard for my children when we first came here. They didn't want to learn English; they wanted to go and live in Guatemala. That's when I explained to them that the government — it calls itself democratic — is not really working in the people's interests. It's tied to the army, and it's responsible for many murders, including their father's. I tell my children never to be ashamed of their father, if someone says he was a guerrilla or something. He'd been fighting for a just cause. He died because he was a person who cared a lot about other human beings. Now, the oldest tells me when he's older he's going to do what his father was doing.

While the army is still in control, I won't go back. Nothing's really changed under the new government. The disappearances and assassinations continue: my brother was murdered in November 1986. Nothing's going to change in Guatemala until there's been a victory by the people.

We all have to work hard, though, even if we're not in the country. That's the only way we're going to win power from these murderers. Maybe we won't see it, but our children will.

I Had to Fight for My Sister and Brother

Mariela,
Runujel Junam Council
of Ethnic Communities (CERJ)

My name is Mariela. I'm from a small village in Chiché township, in El Quiché. I began to work in this organization because of our community's needs. Nobody forced me — I'm a woman who likes to work, especially doing this. Right now it's very bad. There are threats everywhere, not just in Chiché. Thank God, in my community it's not too bad. There are threats, but that's not the same as when they make good on them.

I'm the only woman working with this group of young people. In the beginning, I didn't understand much about the roots of the problem, but with experience — especially personal experience — I learned. We have a lot of family problems. Not because there are too many of us. Not because we don't have land. No, we have problems with sickness.

After the violence, my brother and sister were left with emotional problems. The doctors said they're probably incurable. But I wouldn't accept that. I saw my brother and sister were sick, and I went to see other doctors. I went to a "natural" doctor, who charged me seventy *quetzales*. I went to Chichicastenango, to a hospital. The doctor there told me, "This girl is very advanced in her mental illness. I can't cure her. She needs specialists." He gave me some information and an address, and I went to the mental hospital in Guatemala City.

I'd never been to the capital. One Sunday, I went to look for the hospital. I didn't bring my sister — it was too hard to travel with her. I talked to a social worker and told her my problem. She told me, "You must bring your sister here for the doctors to see." Now I knew where to go, who to talk to. I didn't have any money, but my parents and I collected a little, and then I went with my sister. They gave me some medicine and told me to come back if she didn't get better. She stayed the same.

She complains a lot about her head: "My head hurts. I feel like people are talking to me, like I have something heavy here. I hear noises. They're screaming at me." She still does this. She can't stand to see men — she runs away from men, even from my brother.

Before the violence, when she was about eight or nine, she was a very lively little girl. She liked to go out to the country, where it was quiet, to pick fruit to sell in the market. One day she was out with her basket and some boys came up, about the same age as her, ten or eleven. Then they chased her; she fell. They grabbed her, took off her clothes, and they raped her.

She should have said something, but she was afraid. She thought that if she said anything she'd be kicked out of the house, that maybe it was her fault. Nobody knew what had happened. Then the violence came.

My sister was already sick, but she didn't show it very much. At the time I wasn't at home; I was working in the departmental capital. My family had to leave home. There were days when they ate and days when they didn't. You had to keep moving, so you don't fall in the army's hands. It's like when you mop the floor: everything is mopped away. That's how the army acts.

Bodies were dumped everywhere — people didn't know

where to run to. Like it or not, my sister's nerves were destroyed, seeing so many bodies, maybe walking over them. Sometimes there was no room on the path and you had to jump over the bodies and move on. The dead had been tortured, raped. There were old people, women, just dumped on the ground.

So after the violence she was much worse. She was furious. She'd go out alone at night; she wasn't afraid of the dark. She says when she's asleep she has a lot of nightmares. So what she does is avoid sleep. When she sleeps she sees people, people who were killed by the army. They talk to her: "Come with us," they say. And they grab her and they pick her up and carry her. When she wakes up she's very frightened, and her mind begins to work, but in a bad way.

At the hospital they haven't been able to do anything for her. In the beginning, they helped me by paying for half of her medication, but then they stopped. And I can't pay anymore.

I'm the oldest; I'm the one that does everything. I feel sick sometimes. My morale gets low. Sometimes I don't want to do anything. I want to run away from these sicknesses. But I begin to think: what will happen to them when they no longer have my help? My mother suffers the most because she's constantly with the two sick ones. My mother is malnourished, very thin. Sometimes she doesn't even feel like eating.

It's because of the violence that my brother's like he is. If there hadn't been any violence, I'm sure that they wouldn't have gotten so sick. Thank God, there were some Spanish nuns who helped with him. My brother tries to work a little; he helps out at the nuns' house, and they help with his medication.

My brother's sick, and they forced him to take part in the Patrols.[10] It's not enough he's mentally ill, they wanted him to work with them too. Then when we heard you could do something to avoid this — get rid of them — we came together with a group of young people and talked. What should we do? I had to do something. I had to fight for my sister and brother. It wasn't right to force him to patrol.

People came to us little by little until we formed a huge group. And then, when people voted on the leadership, they proposed my name. I became the secretary. That was July 31, 1988, the day our organization was born. Now there are six thousand of us in CERJ. CERJ influences a lot of people.

The army is very aware that the organization is big and that it's a legal organization. They don't want the patrols to end because they want them to do their dirty work; they don't want to do the mass killings themselves. Now, many communities no longer have patrols. The army goes from community to community, accusing community or union organizations of being subversive and saying the violence will return. That's our biggest problem. They say mass killings and violence ended because of the patrols: "The past will return." That's what they say. "We know the organizations in the community. It's because you let these people in, because of these organizations the violence returns."

Our goal is to work not just with the civil patrol, but to work with widows, with the poorest people. That's what we want.

Talking to the Authorities is
Like Talking to a Rock

Emilia García,
Mutual Support Group (GAM)

My name is Emilia García. I'm the mother of Edgar Fernando García, who disappeared February 18, 1984. He was kidnapped on the street by members of the BROE.[11] They forced him into a car and took him away to an unknown destination. There were witnesses. Some people noticed what was happening, but they were afraid to say what they'd seen. But they came to us and told us what had happened. Nothing we've done to find him has made any difference.

He worked at the CAVISA[12] glass factory, where he was in the executive of the union. There's no doubt that's why they took him away. That was his crime. At the time they were fighting for a collective agreement, and he was constantly going to the Ministry of Labour. When they picked him up it was just a few days before the contract was supposed to be signed.

Disappearances are terrible. You always have your mind fixed, wondering what has happened to your child, above all because you know that these people use barbaric methods. You don't know where he is, or who has him. You're going around, asking, and nobody tells you anything. Even if they know, they don't give out any information about the disappeared.

As we were going around looking for him, we met several people who had the same problem. We started to get to know each other. We came together, thinking that if we were united, maybe we could put greater pressure on the authorities. But talking to the authorities is like talking to a rock: they aren't moved by anything. Although there were a lot of us, they never gave us any answers about any of our family members.

As a group, we went public on June 4, 1984. After that, a lot of people joined. In the beginning, there were only those of us from here in the capital. But as the news spread across the country, people came from many places: from El Quiché, Chimaltenango, Suchitepéquez, Escuintla, El Petén, Santa Rosa, from all over Alta Verapaz and Baja Verapaz — from almost all departments. That's how we began the struggle, not just for our family members but against all human rights violations in Guatemala.

We thought the situation was going to improve, at least a little bit, with the change in government. But in spite of our struggle, there are still terrible human rights violations. All that's changed is that the president is no longer in uniform; he's a civilian. But the military is still around. There are so many widows. So many women whose husbands have disappeared. So many children abandoned — orphans without anyone to care for them. And even now the army calls them "guerrillas." They say young children are guerrillas.

The president says we should forget the past. But it's impossible for us to forget a past so cruel. It's always the present for us. Even if the situation were to change, we would never forget our families. In a war, there are many dead. But war has never been declared here.

Nothing's changed. In no way has the situation improved. Economically, we're in bad shape. Everything is very expensive, wages cover nothing. Education is bad. The schools are poorly looked after. No attention is paid to people's health. The most basic human rights are constantly violated.

Here only the people can bring change, through constant

struggle. But it's going to be very difficult, and it's going to cost many more lives too. Nothing can change in Guatemala until the people feel there is at least respect for life.

Don't Be Fooled by What the President Says

Linda Neomí,
Mutual Support Group (GAM)

My name is Linda Neomí. I come from San Juan Comalapa, in Chimaltenango. We're Cakchiquel — that's our language. My story's a long one, and I'm only telling part of it. We live here in the capital, because of the violence. In the 1980s, there was a lot of violence. And in 1981 they took my father away. We were left with absolutely nothing.

We'd escaped to the capital in 1980, because we were told they were looking for my father. He couldn't find work here, and one day he said he was going back to the village to see a man who owed him some money — we didn't have enough for supper. He didn't come back. They took him down to the military base, and my mother's been looking for him ever since. She's done everything. She even went to the base, but they never give us any answers.

Since then we've been alone. With nothing. There are four of us and my mother. It was very hard because we were very young. My oldest sister was twelve and I was eight. We couldn't work. My mother couldn't either. She had a lot of emotional problems, so she lost her will to work.

Because we couldn't pay for our room and all the rest anymore we went back to the village. But when we got back there were rumours floating around that what had happened to our father was going to happen to us, so we came back to the capital, in 1982.

My youngest brother started working in the markets, carting water. I did that too. They paid us very little — two cents a jug, fifteen to twenty-five cents a day. It was so little, but because they gave us lunch it helped my mother. She began to work in a tortilla factory. She ground 100 kilograms of corn into tortillas every day. They paid her very little, but we managed to get by.

I began to work with GAM in 1988. We couldn't find any way out of our problems. And we needed my father. Then we heard about GAM. Because of my pain I wanted to work, to help the group. I began to work as the monitor of the literacy program. We teach people in the group. Most of them don't know how to read or write, and they can't speak Spanish. They can't express themselves and there are problems during meetings. So we decided to teach them. It was a way out for me because I didn't have a job, no way to keep clothes on my back, no way to help my mother.

Ours is a very long struggle. GAM's members live with great pain. But it's because of our pain that we've achieved what we have. Still, we have a lot of problems, most of them economic. Most of us are wives and children. They've taken away husbands and fathers, and this has affected us emotionally and economically.

Don't be fooled by what the president says — that there's no more violence, or anything like that. Guatemalans who live here know there are still human rights violations, even if they say otherwise. We know very well what violence and discrimination mean.

All We Have Now
Is a Bitter Memory

María,
Mutual Support Group (GAM)

My name is María. I'm from the town of Santa Cruz del Quiché. One of my brothers was murdered in 1982, and another was kidnapped about thirty days later.

I joined GAM because of my father. He's sick. His hearing is impaired. But he listens to all the news on the radio, and he heard about GAM. He didn't have any idea what it was, but he heard that it was in Zone Eleven. So he went, but the first time he got lost. He asked directions, but because he couldn't hear it didn't make any difference. Then the second time he found it. But he didn't understand. So he came home and told me, "There's this group, but I can't hear what they're saying. Maybe you could come with me because I'd really like to know where my son is and where the others who are missing are. Even if they just show us their bones, we want to see them."

My brother was picked up by the army. They were surrounding the village where we lived. At the time he was living with his father-in-law. They'd just killed my other brother. So he said he was going to visit my mother to see how she was. The army took him. They said he had to be in custody for forty-eight hours. To this day, we don't know anything. And the army and the treasury police killed the other one — he was working, cutting corn. It was December, harvest time, and he was out working in the fields. They shot him right there. All we have now is a bitter memory.

For more than three years I've been living and working

here in the capital. This group has achieved so much. They've managed to recover a lot of bodies from clandestine cemeteries. If it weren't for GAM, the army wouldn't let us work.

Before I didn't have a stable place. I came and went because of the worry and fear. So many other things have happened in the village. And now they know in the village that I'm working with GAM. They say people in GAM are guerrillas. But it isn't like that.

Endnotes

1. Interviews with Guatemalan women, March and April 1991.
2. *Americas Watch: The Group for Mutual Support (1984–1985)* (New York/Washington: Americas Watch Committee, 1985), p. 2.
3. Women from the department of San Marcos, Patrullas de Auto-defensa Civil en Guatemala: Entre la división y resistencia de las comunidades indígenas, Centro Exterior de Reportes Informativos Sobre Guatemala, CERIGUA, Oct. 3, 1991, Mexico, p. 1.
4. Inter-Church Committee on Human Rights in Latin America, *Annual Report* (1990), p. 12.
5. Cerezo was elected in 1985, in elections financed partially by the U.S. government.
6. Civil Patrols.
7. Since GAM began the campaign to disclose the location of clandestine cemetaries hundreds of bodies have been found. CONAVIGUA has also played a crucial role in this campaign.

8. Canada has been criticized at home and abroad for requiring all Guatemalans wanting to travel to Canada to have visas, ostensibly to prevent false refugees claims. Applying for a visa or for refugee status from within Guatemala can itself put the applicant at risk. Beatríz Barrios Marroquín, who had been kidnapped previously by the death squads, was murdered after visiting the Embassy. She was kidnapped the second time on December 10, 1985. Her body was found on December 14, 1985.

9. Unlike most European governments, the Canadian government does not have refugee reception centres. In general, refugees are housed in modest hotels until they find private accommodation.

10. Civil Patrols.

11. The Brigadas de Operaciones Especiales (BROE) are the special operations brigades of the National Police. Although they are officially responsible for crowd control, they are notorious for their connections to the death squads.

12. CAVISA refers to the Industria Centroamericana de Vidrios, Socieded Anonima, Glass Industry of Central America, Ltd.

In memory of Yolanda Urízar —

Union advisor and a member of the CNT, a national labour federation, Yolanda Urízar continued her work long after most labour leaders had been killed or forced into exile. In March 1983, she was kidnapped and is still missing.

CHAPTER FOUR

Women and the Unions

In 1991, one quarter of Guatemalan women worked for a wage.[1] However, the unionized waged work force is very small, and fewer than 9 percent of these women belong to a union.[2] But women working in the unions are standing up to their employers and challenging their male counterparts on women's role in the union and in society. And as in any industry in any country, even where the work force is entirely male, pro-longed strikes that do not have the strong support of strikers' wives, daughters, sisters and mothers stand very little chance of success.

The union movement made little headway until the Ten Years of Spring, between 1944 and 1954.[3] Dockworkers from the United Fruit Company and other workers had earlier waged illegal strikes, but these were put down by soldiers and government security forces.

During the Ten Years of Spring, unions won the right to organize. A new labour code, introduced in 1947, guaranteed the eight-hour day, a minimum wage and other benefits, and lifted the ban on rural unions. Women had begun to enter the paid work force, and special labour laws were enacted to support working women. The coup in June 1954 brought an abrupt end to organizing, and unionists were among the thousands who were killed or forced into exile.

New attempts to organize workers were made in the 1960s, but it was not until 1973 that union organizing mushroomed again. That year teachers went on a strike which lasted several months and spread across the nation. Their strike was successful, and wages were raised 25 percent. Sparked by the teachers' success, the drive for unionization was on again.[4]

Union organizing is a hazardous occupation. First, fellow workers must be persuaded that the union is worth the risk. Organizers face many obstacles: a Labour Ministry that blocks workers at every turn, recalcitrant owners (both national and foreign), security forces that protect the elite at any cost, using the now well-known methods of threats, beatings, kidnappings and assassinations.

But by 1976, several unions were either forming or in conflict with the employer. Factory owners, taking advantage of the chaos caused by the earthquake in February of that year, tried to destroy unions. On March 24, 1976, 152 workers at the Coca Cola bottling plant were fired. Workers occupied the factory. Franchise owner John Trotter called in the security forces. That night they brutally evicted the workers, seriously injuring twelve and arresting another fourteen.[5]

Solidarity with the workers at Coca Cola was strong and reaction swift. A meeting of over sixty unions resulted in the creation of the National Committee of Trade Union Unity (CNUS) — a name taken from an organization formed shortly after the 1954 coup. As the CNUS grew stronger, the government was forced to recognize the union at Coca Cola.[6] Other labour-management conflicts broke out at banks, bus companies, sugar refineries, mines and textile plants.

If forming a union is difficult, women working in industry face additional obstacles in their efforts to organize: lack of time and lack of support from partners and co-workers. As one woman worker puts it, "It's hard for me to participate because of my children. My husband doesn't want me to participate anyway. He wants me to devote myself to the kids. And they shut down the factory where I worked, so I stay at home."[7]

A few of the unions organized in the 1970s were in plants where most of the workers were women. The workers at Industrias Acrilicas de Centroamerica, Sociedad Anonima, (Acrylic Industries of Central America Ltd.) were 90 percent women. In 1977, the women at ACRICASA

> ...decided to carry out a work stoppage to demand the signing of a collective agreement covering working conditions and putting an end to company reprisals. For fourteen days they occupied the plant, sleeping, eating and conducting meetings there. On the third day, riot police showed up at the request of the owners. When workers noticed the police, they started the machines and began to work. The police, who thought they were going to find evidence of a strike and evict the workers, had to leave... From then on, the owners and main supervisors refused to enter the plant, leaving it without technical or administrative management. The workers decided to continue working for the next eleven days, until raw materials were used up. Finally, the owners ... forced the workers to take vacation. During the next ten working days production remained at a standstill. When the workers returned to their jobs, the company began ending contracts on the basis of the "illegal work stoppage."[8]

The government's response to the growing strength of

organized workers was to force union leaders into exile or kill them. On May Day in 1980, dozens of protesters were kidnapped. On June 21, 1980, in broad daylight, the national police kidnapped twenty-seven leaders of the National Workers' Federation (CNT). In a similar kidnapping on August 24th of the same year, seventeen leaders of the CNT vanished from a religious retreat centre near Guatemala City. Eight of the kidnapped unionists are women. All are still missing. The CNT and the CNUS disappeared. Those unionists remaining fled the country or went underground.

In 1983 union organizing was made legal again. And again Coca Cola workers took the lead. After the franchise owners abandoned the plant, workers occupied their factory from February 1984 until February 1985 to make sure that the equipment was not removed. They won their struggle, and today their union is one of the strongest in Guatemala.

Following a slight easing of repression in the mid-eighties, the Union of Guatemalan Workers (UNSITRAGUA) was formed in February 1985, bringing together some of the unions that had been active in the CNUS. UNSITRAGUA then helped to found Labour and Popular Action Unity (UASP) in 1987. In February 1991, more than one hundred labour organizations came together in the Guatemalan Workers' Unitarian Front (FUTG). The new federation includes city workers and rural workers from the south coast, the northeast and the northern department of El Petén. Its affiliates include bank workers, public sector workers and workers at the beer factory.

Guatemalan unions in the 1990s face the same problems as their predecessors, but there are new problems too, such as the introduction of *solidarista* associations[9] and the spread of *maquila* industries.

Solidarista associations are part of a union-busting strategy that has been very successful in other Central American countries, particularly in Costa Rica. According to the plan, workers participate with management instead of being in conflict with it — cooperation for the common good. Workers can invest in their companies and are entitled to certain benefits. Supported by national business and by the United States government, Guatemala is now the prime target for the growth of *solidarista* associations that cut away at the base of independent union support and squeeze out more from each worker.

Another challenge to the union movement is the growth of the *maquila* industries. *Maquilas* are foreign-owned factories on Guatemalan soil, exempt from national taxes and not bound by troublesome labour laws. Companies have parts shipped to Guatemala, where they are assembled. The finished product is then sent back to the international market. *Maquilas* are notorious for their poor pay, unbearable working conditions and owners with strong anti-union sentiments. *Maquila* factories are concentrated in the textile industry, where most workers are women.

Unions had traditionally been difficult places for women to participate. This is beginning to change, especially as union women come together for the first time in their own organizations. The Women's Group for the Betterment of the Family (GRUFEPROMEFAM) was formed in 1986 and includes women unionists and the wives of organized men. COMFUITAG is the Women's Group at the International Union of Food and Allied Workers' Associations, which unites thirteen unions, including the Coca Cola workers. These groups are the first among union organizations to address seriously women's participation and to create an opening for discussion between men and women and among women themselves.

My Choice Could Have Been to Serve the System

*Marta Gloria Torres,
United Representation of the
Guatemalan Opposition*

Various reasons, usually very concrete ones, motivate women to participate in the struggle. Perhaps one has to do with children. When I was still in Guatemala, I thought, "What's the use devoting myself only to taking care of my children? When they're fifteen or twenty, they're going to turn up at the side of the road, tortured. Who could guarantee that they weren't going to do this to one or more of my children?" It's this kind of reasoning that, in the long run, leads many women to join.

When I was young it would startle me to see malnourished children in the streets, children sleeping on the sidewalk, covered with newspapers, or women with children in their arms, begging. But even being startled by this situation is a step forward in a society like Guatemala — you can become so numb you begin to think this kind of life is normal.

I was privileged because I had options, but my choice could have been to serve the system — to become very rich, to devote myself to myself and my family. That could have been my path, but I chose to walk the other way. It wasn't the result of a single decision, but rather a series of steps leading to other doors. Other compañeras, no longer with us, had a very clear vision — they were completely clear that their commitment could cost them their lives. They knew the consequences — not that they wanted to be martyrs — but they thought their lives could benefit others. In this sense, I think we're all given chances in life, and our decisions lead us down one path or another.

I studied law for six years in university. I had a very comfortable life; I liked to party. I lived an upper-middle-class life, but at the same time I knew what was happening on the streets of Guatemala. I realized while I'd made it to university, there were fifty thousand young people who hadn't had that chance — it hadn't been a personal triumph for me. I'd gone a step further, but it was my responsibility to translate this into serving the people. For a while I practiced civil law with some friends, but I really didn't like it. I felt I'd wasted my time studying law because it's a mockery, and because of the obscene corruption in Guatemala. Then I began to work for the CNT, the National Workers' Federation. Only then did those years of study make sense.

When we began in 1975, they didn't have lawyers. Nobody wanted to work as a labour lawyer. I was married and I'd just had my third daughter. Enrique[10] and I and others began to advise emerging unions. Some came to have a history of intense struggle, including the miners in Ixtahuacán, the workers at the Coca Cola bottling plant and the women at the ACRICASA textile factory.

In Guatemala, workers are disposable. That's the level industrial brutality and dehumanization have reached in our country. More attention is paid to the machinery than to the workers. The workers are just replaceable parts in production. It's always been that way. Unions began to form after the first quarter of this century, as people became aware of what they had in common: their exploitation as workers.

In the period from 1944 to 1954, union organizing reached a tremendous peak, although neither the workers nor the campesinos participated in the overthrow of Ubico.[11] It wasn't a completely democratic period — they were just beginning to get to the roots of injustice. It was an evolution towards a socioeconomic system that would have been more just for most Guatemalans. In our country, people don't have an education, but they know when they see a chance for real change, and workers and campesinos were becoming part of that process.

Unions flourished in that period. In the 1970s, the percentage of organized workers didn't rise above 7 percent of the economically active population, but between 1944 and 1954, 20 percent of the workers were organized.[12]

In 1954, following the CIA invasion and the overthrow of Arbenz, most unions were destroyed. It was selective terror. Most leaders of worker and campesino organizations were killed. They said unions were synonymous with the government of Arbenz, and the government of Arbenz was synonymous with communism.

People were terrorized. Five thousand members and leaders of grassroots groups were killed. The period from 1954 to 1973 was like the aftermath of a bad injury. First people had to assimilate what had happened, why it had happened, who had benefitted from it and what mistakes had been made. But human beings have a collective memory. Very few unions were formed during those twenty years and those that did were controlled.

But in the 1970s the union movement began to grow again. When we began to work for the CNT there were six labour-management conflicts; four years later there were fifty-six. It was a time without precedent. When the workers in the March of the Ixtahuacán Miners reached the capital, for example, it inspired not only people there; it also raised the awareness of people they met along the way.

The Ixtahuacán mine was in rural Huehuetenango. Many of the people who worked in the mine were campesinos. They received very low wages, and most had respiratory problems. Many had tuberculosis — if a worker had a cough, they fired him. The company decided to close down when it saw the union being organized there was militant. They were going to close the mines to destroy the union and then reopen them. So the miners decided to march on the capital.

This march caused a furor throughout the country. People left their villages to join the marchers. It began on a Friday, and on Sunday, we were close to Quetzaltenango. I was overwhelmed — I'd never seen such an enormous response from the public. The approach to Quetzaltenango is very straight, and the streets were filled with pots overflowing with *chuchitos*,[13] tamales, fruit drinks, coffee. More than four thousand *quetzales* were collected, in one-cent, five-cent or ten-cent coins. The poor accountant at CNT spent days counting that money. Everywhere people were organizing solidarity activities.

People in the markets didn't have money but brought fruit and vegetables. What moved me more than anything was when a young woman came into the CNT with an old rag covering something. The cloth was so old, but it was well-washed, and white. Underneath was a huge pile of refried beans — from the people in one of the poorest neighbourhoods in the city.

The march was like an ocean wave, impossible to control. When it reached the capital it was one hundred thousand strong. Thousands of other people had joined along the way but hadn't made it to the capital. Workers came into the city with their feet bleeding, and the public responded. They were in the streets singing and shouting. When Donaldo Alvarez[14] appeared on the balcony of the National Palace thousands of people stood and shouted, "Assassin! Assassin!" It was the first time since the 1950s that so many people had come together.

Something that's not talked about is the role the miners' wives played. When the workers left on the march the women stayed behind and guarded the mine because the company wanted to remove all the machinery and close it down. One woman, I remember, had a baby twenty days old, and they had gone to block the mine entrance. The town of Ixtahuacán was about four kilometres away. One day the owners came with their lawyers and the police; the women formed a line, and they wouldn't let them cross.

Another important case we worked on was for the union at the Coca Cola bottling plant. The struggle there lasted more than a decade and cost several lives. I remember when John Trotter, the owner of the plant, came to Guatemala. The workers were camped out on the street after they had been violently thrown out of the factory for protesting the firing of union leaders.

Trotter came in to the office, screaming at us like he ran the world, not just the factory! He stood up by the window and he shouted at the workers in English, "Get out of here! All of you! If you don't get out, I've got enough power with the army and the MLN[15] to have you thrown out by force." We translated what he said. And Pedro Quevedo[16] responded in a voice that was stronger and louder: "No, we're not moving. Not one of us." And the gringo turned around, pale and startled. I could see his face. And Pedro continued, "And we're not afraid of you." The gringo looked so shocked.

This was very important because it reflected what the United States has done with us in Latin America. The situation in Central America is largely created by the United States, and that's why the union movement is so important: that's the arena of serious confrontation between the United States — which is used to controlling people's lives — and the workers themselves. What vision do those who control the world have? They don't recognize borders; they don't know what social justice means; they don't care if a mother doesn't have enough to feed her child. That's not the language transnationals understand. They speak a different language and that's profit, whatever the cost.

It was the first time a union had stood up and said no. And this is what changed the entire situation of unions in our country. Coca Cola was a catalyst. Workers all over the country began to see the need for a strong organized workers' movement.

The situation for women working in industry is very difficult. Working conditions are deplorable, but if a woman doesn't accept them, there are fifty women behind her, applying for the same job. Many women are single mothers. If you look at the Guatemalan Labour Code, there's a section on women and work. It states that women don't have to work the night shift, that women have the right to a fifteen-minute break every two hours to nurse their infants. The law says that where there are more than twenty women working in a factory, the company has to set up a daycare centre. Very good laws, but almost no one obeys them.

At ACRICASA, a Japanese textile company where about 90

percent of the workers were women, they began to organize a union. The owners didn't want to set up a child-care centre. They said they had to get established first; when there was a profit then something could be done. The workers didn't accept this.

The situation inside of this factory was incredibly difficult. I remember one day we arrived and there was a woman about seven or eight months pregnant — it was about seven in the morning and she had been working since ten the night before. Workers have to be standing all the time, walking, so the threads won't get caught. When I asked for a chair for this woman I was told that chairs were prohibited. Back then they earned $2.04 a day, but after deductions they got about $56 a month. Paying someone to take care of the children, paying for transportation, food, and being single mothers — it was incredible!

Finally one compañera, Sonia, who was on the union executive — she had a child. She said she was going to bring him to the factory and she was going to leave him there. That's how, after three years, the fight was won. Finally they opened a little room, with two or three cribs and playpens, but in the beginning the women didn't want to leave their children there — they were afraid of the bosses. They thought they might kill the children or poison them. Sonia was the first. Once when they wanted to pressure her because of her union involvement — she went to pick up her nine-month-old baby — and they said they wouldn't give him to her. So she said, "Fine, don't give him to me." And she left the child all night.

For many reasons, it's very difficult to organize women. We haven't been brought up to take initiatives, let alone at the political level. There are also a lot of problems at home for married women. For men it's easier. He can say, "Tonight I've got a union meeting," and off he goes while she stays with the children. But a woman can't just say, "I'm going to a union meeting." She has to take her children with her or find someone to look after them. If her husband is supportive then there aren't any other problems, but if he isn't, then she has to sneak out to meetings. A lot of women did that.

On the other hand, many women didn't get the support of male workers, even when they were unionized. With everything combined, and considering the exhaustion so many women feel, it's very difficult for a woman to take on leadership positions in a union.

When I began to work at the CNT it wasn't easy. I think we were the first women who worked advising a labour federation. Women had been in the unions, but not in the federations. It was difficult in the beginning — the mentality in Guatemala is that only men can do the most difficult work, both physical work and intellectual work. So they thought that if men couldn't do union work, how could a woman? When the workers saw that their advisor was a woman they reacted with worry, sadness, despair. But over the years, people got to know us, and then they even began to look for women advisors.

By 1977 Enrique and I were working with the miners of Ixtahuacán, Coca Cola, and ACRICASA, and we had fifteen other cases as well. It was a time of intense activity for the CNT, with all the cases being very serious ones. Towards the end we knew repression was coming. We'd heard rumours there was a list with more than a thousand names, people in grassroots groups who were going to be hit by the repression.

The situation was getting worse every day, but I didn't think that it was going to happen so fast. We had already received threats at the CNT and at home on the phone. There were always people out front, watching. On March 3, 1977, we were leaving the CNT by car when a car from the Ministry of the Interior ran us off the road. Enrique and I were injured. In Ixtahuacán the bosses began to celebrate because at first the news was that we'd been killed.

That night I had one of the most difficult realizations that can come to a person: to know that another human being, just like yourself, wants to take your life, feels he has the right to take it. That night I would have liked to have spoken, without hatred, with those who ordered the attack.

They hadn't planned to get just one of us — it was the whole union movement. That was the signal. Later we heard from someone who'd been at the meeting that people from CACIF[17] had decided to kill Mario López Larrave,[18] Quique[19] and me. Mario was killed on June 8th that year. They thought that by killing labour advisors they could kill the union movement. I was afraid. But, on the other hand, I thought that my life shouldn't be controlled by fear: as the Mothers of the Plaza de Mayo[20] say, fear is a prison without bars. And I didn't want to live imprisoned by my fear.

Throughout 1977 and 1978 there were different kinds of threats. We stayed for two years after the assassination attempt. We kept doing the same work — the truth is we thought we'd go on as long as we could. At the same time, repression exploded throughout the union movement. They began to strike at grassroots leaders. As a movement we tried to resist, but unarmed it's very difficult to resist Guatemalan military brutality. Several compañeras were picked up and held.

In 1978 a list was published in the newspaper. I'd just had Andrea.[21] About three weeks earlier the two compañeras who worked as secretaries at the CNT talked to me and begged me not to come to the office anymore. They thought if the security forces wanted to terrorize the union movement even more than they already had, a pregnant woman would be the perfect target. They'd noticed a man taking photos of me — many, many photos — and I hadn't seen him. I am so grateful to these women. Without saying anything to anybody, I simply stopped going to the office. I hid at home.

When Andrea was born the list came out. I remember she was born at two or three in the afternoon, but a compañero was talking with me at noon about some problems with a case we were working on. It was so difficult to concentrate on having that child and at the same time on paying attention to the problems with our cases!

The list came out less than forty-eight hours after she was born. They started killing people, beginning with Oliverio Castañeda de Leon.[22] My doctor came and told me, "I think they might come here and kill you. You'd better get out of here today." I left the three older girls with my mother, Quique went somewhere else, and I went into hiding. I was moving almost every night, and with a two-day-old baby — it was horrible. There's a place I remember, full of spider webs and dust — it was like a horror movie. I was thinking Andrea was going to die. The time came when I had nowhere to go. This went on for a month and a half, and then we fled the country. That was in December of 1978.

Being forced to leave is one of the most humiliating things that can happen to a human being. Being thrown out of your home is traumatizing; imagine being thrown out of your country. They haven't tried to destroy Guatemalans just by murdering, making us disappear and torturing us — they've tried to destroy our will to defend our dignity, freedom, basic values, desires. Exile is one way. Many people can't take exile — it's not easy. But we're still part of the Guatemalan process. We play a different role than we did when we were inside the country.

It's taken time for us to understand this, but it's an important role, especially now that international matters are important to the government. Exile is only bearable to the degree that you don't forget why it happened, who made it happen; and to the degree that you don't forget those who are still in your homeland, to the degree that you're part of the people, although far away. This makes exile bearable, and exile gives you energy that can be channelled.

When we left, Yoly[23] took over our cases, including the Coca Cola workers. It was just after they killed Pedro Quevedo, the General Secretary of the Coca Cola Workers' Union. She survived two group kidnappings in 1980, the first at the CNT offices on June 21st, and the second at a religious retreat centre in August. Between the two, forty-four labour leaders were kidnapped.

Then Yoly's daughter was kidnapped. She was held for two weeks and she was tortured. She was sixteen and she was raped by thirty policemen. The first was Manuel de Jesús Valiente Téllez, the chief of the *judiciales*. Something that struck me deeply was that one week after having raped this girl, he walked down the aisle with his daughter: she was dressed in white — she was getting married.

While Yolandita was being held, the international solidarity movement organized a major campaign for her release. There were thousands of telegrams. That's what finally brought her freedom. When she was released she was blind. They had tortured her with the notorious *capucha de gamesan*, a thick rubber hood with no opening, filled with dangerous chemicals. They hold that over your head and you have no choice but to breathe in the fumes. While she was still blind, a group of workers from the south coast, had collected, at tremendous sacrifice, two hundred *quetzales* and sent it to her so she could buy a braille watch. Yolandita thanked them and told them she wasn't going to buy the watch. She was determined to regain her sight, and she gave the money to continue union work. She did get her sight back.

While Yoly's daughter was being held, Yoly kept working with the unions. After her release they worked together. In March of 1983, while General Efraín Ríos Montt was in power, Yolanda disappeared. We still don't know what happened to her. There are rumours — some saying that she was killed and others saying no. Only the army knows the truth.

Of the whole family only Yolandita[24] was left. She wanted to find her mother, and she contacted international organizations, but nothing could be done.

I remember at the time of Yolandita's disappearance, we received a tape that Yoly had made, where she condemned her daughter's kidnapping. She finished with: "We have reason to hate the army, but the love we feel for the people keeps us struggling, and because of this love, we're going to keep on fighting."

Women have always participated. It's difficult for a woman to make that decision, but when she does, she doesn't hold anything back. Guatemala is a sick society, a society that doesn't care about the sick, the children, the poor. It's a society based on destruction and death. In the end, this destroys everything. This has made us understand that now is the time for women to accept responsibilities. We can no longer remain victims, passively suffering the consequences. What's happening is that different women, in different areas, are coming to the conviction that we have the power to change this society.

But its important to mention that women haven't participated on a wide scale, especially during the 1970s. One characteristic of the women of Guatemala has been to be part of the infrastructure of an unjust society, to suffer the consequences and to have little or nothing to say in decisions that affect us. What's most important about this period is that we're taking initiatives and participating with more awareness. What's motivated this? I think for most women it's because they have been directly affected by institutionalized violence. We see this with the widows and their organization, CONAVIGUA, and with GAM, where most members are women. Just the name of these organizations says a lot about a country. It's amazing that women have had to come together around these acts of violence. My hope is that someday we'll begin to come together to build something new.

Right now the struggle for the women of Guatemala is a struggle for survival, for life, for our children. It's a very difficult struggle, with many obstacles. We have much in common with the women of North America, but we have different ways of doing things, different social contexts and different priorities. It's important to make an effort to understand not just the situation in our own countries, but to see how they are connected at a global level. In our country there's profound injustice, and this has consequences for women. But there is also tremendous injustice at the international level, and that's the way that industrialized countries act towards developing countries.

We have much in common, like the search for peace, but I think we're all coming to understand, in North America and in Central America, that the search for peace isn't something abstract. We're also coming to the conclusion that individually we aren't going to find a solution, that this has to be a collective task. But we can't say we're going to all think the same way or act alike.

We have to learn to maintain mutual respect, searching for understanding, informing ourselves about the different contexts in which we move. We need to have a mature relationship, not a paternalistic one. There are often paternalistic attitudes about the situation in countries like Guatemala, or about other Central American countries, or about the Third World. We *can* develop on our own, but we can't do it if our hands are tied. We're going to do it, and we are doing it, but the situation in our country is the product of centuries of injustice.

It's going to be our responsibility as women not only to search for peace, but to work for the environment.[25] We really are at the threshold of a crisis, an economic crisis mixed with an ecological crisis, because of the abuse and irrational use of both natural and human resources. And when we speak of peace, we're not speaking of peace where poverty and misery are the rule. We're talking about a different kind of peace, something much more than the absence of violence. We're talking about a peace where human beings can live with dignity, to develop themselves as people. In this light, it's important that women in North America not only move forward in their struggle but that they defend their gains because when these gains are lost, we all go backwards.

Right now the women of Guatemala are trying to withstand

the repression. The Guatemalan Army looks strong, but in reality it's weak; it's weak because it carries within itself its own destruction. It's dedicated to destruction, but it's also looking at its final days. This makes it all the more dangerous. It's trying to finish off the workers and the campesino organizations. But in the end it's going to destroy itself.

It's a privilege to be living in these times because we're creating the basis for collective work in the future. In Guatemala, in El Salvador, in Nicaragua — in spite of all of the difficulties — one of the most positive things has been the strengthening of relations between people. This brings me great hope — it's *the* hope. I think we're going to be forced to create new ways of relating, very positive ones. It's true we have a long way to go, but we are going to get there, that's certain.

This Struggle Isn't Just for
Us, It's for Our Daughters Too

Rosa Escobar
and Carmen García,
The Women's Committee
of the International Union
of Food and Allied Workers'
Associations (UITA)[26]

Rosa:

My name is Rosa Marina Escobar, and I'm part of the Women's Committee of UITA. I began to work when I was seventeen, as a secretary at a drug company, where the harassment was very heavy because there was no union.

I worked there over a five-year period. I didn't work because I wanted to, but the economic situation at home was very bad. There are eight children and I'm the youngest. I would have liked to continue studying, but I couldn't.

Company harassment was very strong — they even had television monitors to see if you were wasting time. In the beginning, when you were hungry, at ten in the morning or four in the afternoon, you had to go to the bathroom to drink a cup of coffee. The owner there was a "lady" I remember clearly. To your face, she would affectionately call you "little girl." But behind your back she was vindictive. The wages were very low and the treatment was very bad. When we made a mistake they called us "stupid," or "animal."

While I was there I had a very painful experience. My mother had cancer. They'd called me to come and see her because her condition was critical. She was hemorrhaging a lot. I asked for time off, and they said I wasn't a doctor and that my mother wasn't going to be cured by my visit. So they wouldn't give me permission to leave. A month later my mother died. Even though they wouldn't have given me permission, I went to the wake and to the funeral.

A day later, my sister's father-in-law, who'd lived with us, also died. We were still in mourning. The day my sister's father-in-law was buried they came to tell me to show up at work or be fired.

I began to have more contact with compañeros working in the factory. The way they were treated was horrible. It's still the same. I wanted to organize a union. I wanted to speak out even if they fired me. But because I was expecting a baby, they couldn't do it. According to law, they would have had to pay me for the nine months.

What they did instead was to tell the workers if they talked to me they'd be fired. They put my desk up against a wall. I stopped working for a while, but when my little girl was born our economic situation was shaky again. By then I was pregnant with my second baby. Sometimes we didn't have enough for milk — my husband didn't earn enough. That's why I began to work here in the UITA office. But I had very little idea of unionism or union organizing.

I was a student leader at the Commercial School. That's where I became aware of the repression and that wages were never enough. There were so many deaths, and they were firing people who wanted to organize unions.

Here, because of the economic crisis and the violence, I've become aware of the situation of many compañeras — the situation of women in Guatemala. It affects us all, especially women. There are compañeras whose husbands have disappeared, whose children are missing. At some factories compañeras are mistreated or marginalized in their own unions. Then you realize that only by organizing, or through women's groups, are we going to get to participate and some-day change this situation.

That's how the women's group at UITA began in 1988. It's very new. UITA has been restructuring. There are thirteen organizations: the compañeros from the Wheat Workers in Quetzaltenango, and from TACASA (Tobacco Processing Plant), Coca Cola, and INCASA (Coffee Processing Plant), and others. At some factories covered by UITA most of the workers are women — there are others where there aren't any women. But where there are, women weren't participating in union work. So we thought we'd create this group so women could take part in the union too.

Carmen:
We saw the need to form a women's committee at UITA — women must change because if we change, everything's going to change. We wanted the voices of women workers to be heard. For the unions to grow, for women to participate significantly, we have to have the same rights as men.

Rosa:
We have workshops on ideology and women's oppression. In one workshop, more men participated than women. That was very interesting for us. Most of the compañeros — even the ones on the executives — oppressed their compañeras in some way: they exploited her, they marginalized her. Machismo is very strong here in Guatemala. So at the seminar we discussed the oppression and exploitation of women. You become aware of how the dominant class, the capitalists, use the compañeros

to exploit their compañeras through work in the home. And they become the guardians of the same class that's mistreating the compañeras. It was excellent.

There were compañeros who said, "Yes, you're right. Sometimes I come home from work and I tell my wife to take off my socks. Even if she's spent all day working more than me." A compañero can sell his labour power. But a compañera must work at home too, cooking and doing the housework, reinforcing this chain of exploitation. At the time, the compañeros said they'd like to have this seminar for all the unions and to invite the wives too.

Carmen:
It was very exciting. We wanted to move ahead because we were seeing that it could bear fruit. It was a good experience, even though we were beginners. And being working-class women, we can't express ourselves very well. But nonetheless we do the impossible, so the idea they form about women is good. And we show we can do things well. We're good for more than the home. We can work alongside men.

Rosa:
Even holding the workshops, we faced a bunch of obstacles, even here in UITA. When we wanted to have our first workshop — this was going to be a general seminar — they told us they were going to vote on whether we could hold it. Even though our women's committee was already set up.

Another seminar was at the Coca Cola plant, where the compañeras talked about their problems. There we realized that each organization had its own problems to solve, that each case was distinct.

The Coca Cola union told the compañeras in the union that if they participated in the seminar, they'd be suspended. These compañeros are very macho. That's where we got the idea that the workshops should be mixed, to get everyone's attention.

We hardly ever hold seminars here in our offices. Instead, we go out to the unions because we know the compañeras have a double workload — they have their work at home too. So we try to take advantage of when they're in the factories to make it more accessible to them.

The government says that we're all fine. But the truth is we're really messed over. We need solidarity, protests more than anything. As well, we need to know about other experiences so we can learn more. This struggle isn't just for us, it's for our daughters too. It's only by organizing ourselves that we're going to win what we want.

They Can Pay Eight People's Wages by Selling Just One Skirt

Patricia, Transcontinental

My name is Patricia. I worked at Transcontinental for a year and a half. There were seventeen hundred women workers in all. At the factory we made skirts, pants, shirts — for export to the United States. They made enough every day to pay all the workers for a month. Our wages were low — we earned forty-five *quetzales* every two weeks. The minimum wage was 110 *quetzales* a month, but after deductions, we took home ninety a month. That hardly covers anything. Most of us are single mothers. I'm a single mother with two children.

Once, we didn't receive our full pay; we decided to have a wildcat strike. Then they said they'd deduct money. That was when we began to have wildcat after wildcat to make them give us our full pay. When they saw us on strike, I guess they got angry, and they said they were going to fire people — they were going to close the factory.

They began to take out the machinery — they said they had to clean it because it was dirty and that it was being kept in the warehouse. Then they fired a general manager — he'd practically *told* us to get involved in the union, and quick, because it would be on our side. If we didn't, we were going to end up with almost nothing.

That's how we began to organize the union. We told the whole factory and asked workers to help us because the factory was going to shut down — they weren't going to give any benefits to anybody.

Then the bosses began to demand that people hand in

letters of resignation. They were firing people, making offers. First they were going to give them 25 percent; then they said they were going to give 50 percent, then 75 percent. Then they said they were going to give 100 percent of the benefits. But it was all lies — they never gave them their money. That was how they were getting rid of people — so we wouldn't have a majority. After all these people quit only 460 remained.

The factory shut down on September 23rd. They gave us a holiday, three days off. And during those three days they took out more machinery, practically all of it. When we came back to work, they had chosen people who weren't with us to go in and work. Most of us remained on the street. We already had a mediator, so we could get inside the factory again. That's when we finally took over the plant. We wouldn't leave. There were almost 460 women in the beginning; some of them brought their children with them.

The unions began to come out in solidarity with us. UNSITRAGUA, Coca Cola, they brought us help. Lunafil, Capri too. While we were living there, they brought us food.

The occupation lasted for seven months. In February, the owner of the Víctor Battery Factory — he was also the owner of the land this factory was on — said he had to see about renting it. He had us thrown out, and we stayed on the street for nearly twenty days.

It looks like the man who was acting as the owner was only the representative of the real owners, who are in New York. But people in charge here — we haven't seen any of them. They disappeared. One was Israeli and the others were Filipinos. And up to now the government hasn't done anything for us. Two compañeros who were helping us — they were negotiating for us — managed to talk with the owners in New

York. They sent some help — when they left they didn't pay vacation pay, or even wages. Nothing. Absolutely nothing.

There are sixty-five compañeras in the fight. Most had to leave. We produced clothing that people in North America use — the brand name is Liz Claiborne. One of the skirts we make here sells there at a very high price — they can pay eight people's wages by selling just one skirt. It would be better not to buy so much clothing from these companies — the clothes they sell are made by exploiting poor people in countries like ours.

Someday We're Going to Get What We Want

Thelma

My name is Thelma. I began working when I was twenty-six years old, after I was widowed. Feeling the need to be organized, I joined the union a year and a half later.

When I began I worked as a cleaner. A year later they promoted me to packer; they could see I wanted to learn and better myself, and very soon they gave me an operator's job. Now I work as a machine operator.

Soon the company began to harass us, and I went on the union executive. In order to do that I had to go to Mexico to take a course. It was very good; I gained a lot of experience, although I had to leave my daughters alone. When I came back I had to marry off the older one. These things just happen and we have to get on with the struggle.

There are only two women on my union's executive. What we want is for all the women to get active. We don't dislike men; we want to work alongside them so they'll realize we're equal, that we should struggle together so someday we'll be truly united.

Now they realize we shouldn't be discriminated against. At least the compañeros on the executive have come to understand that women should be allowed to participate. A woman has a lot of problems working on the executive because she has to do practically twice the work: working at her job and working at home, taking care of the children.

When you leave the factory you come home and do the housework, and then those of us who are on the executive practically have three jobs — at the factory, at home and then on the executive. It's really hard, but we've begun to see the fruits of our struggle, and we do whatever we can to keep on working. Someday we're going to get what we want.

Endnotes

1. Data from the National Statistics Institute, 1989.
2. Ibid.
3. With the exception of a brief period in the 1920s, Guatemalan workers had not been free to organize until the Arbenz government. A year before Arbenz was overthrown, nearly 90 percent of the urban work force was organized. After the coup, unions had to submit new lists of officers. No one who had served during the Ten Years of Spring could hold office. By the seventies, fewer than a quarter of the unions active before the coup were still active. See Handy, *Gift of the Devil*, p. 226.
4. Jonas and Tobias, *A NACLA Report*, p. 189.
5. Miguel Angel Albizúrez, *Tiempo de sudor y lucha* (Guatemala City: self-published, 1985), pp. 26–28.
6. Coca Cola workers paid heavily for union recognition. Between 1978 and 1980, eight union leaders were murdered. In a more conventional union-busting tactic, Trotter subdivided operations. Beginning in 1980, a worldwide boycott of Coca Cola, organized by the International Food and Allied Workers' in Geneva and backed by unions and churches, forced the parent company to buy out Trotter's franchise. The franchise owners tried to close the plant again in 1984, claiming

bankruptcy. Workers again occupied the plant. See Barry and Preusch, *Central America Fact Book*, pp. 244–246. During both occupations, Canadian unions and union federations sent money. The Canadian Labour Congress and individual unions also sent delegations to spend time in the plant during the second occupation.

7. *Situación de la mujer en Guatemala IV*, p. 3.

8. Jonathan L. Fried et al., eds., *Guatemala in Rebellion: Unfinished History* (New York: Grove Press, 1983), p. 164.

9. This tactic is very reminiscent of the "team concept," "quality circles," "focus groups" and "management by responsibility" programs now popular with employers worldwide. Workers are urged to become individual "stakeholders," to take on more work for the same pay and, where there is a union, to ignore the collective agreement. Some of the U.S.–based companies using the tactic are Standard Oil of Indiana, McDonald's, Walt Disney Productions, Johnson and Johnson, Time-Life, Polaroid and United Airlines. In Canada the tactic is frequently applied in industry and is now gaining favour with public sector management. Nowhere have these programs shifted power from the employer to the workers.

10. Enrique Torres, also an advisor to the CNT, is Marta Torres' husband.

11. A strong backer of United Fruit and other enterprises, General Jorge Ubico, a wealthy landowner, won the hastily called 1931 elections and held power until 1944.

12. Handy's figure, 90 percent, refers only to urban workers. Torres' figure includes rural workers.

13. *Chuchitos*: corn dumplings, resembling tamales but smaller.
14. Donaldo Alvarez was the much hated Minister of the Interior from 1976–1982 in the governments of Lauguerud García and Lucas García.
15. The MLN (Movimiento de Liberación Nacional, National Liberation Movement) is a far-right political party which boasted of its ties to the death squads. See Handy, *Gift of the Devil*, for details on its activities.
16. The first General Secretary of the Coca Cola Workers' Union, murdered December 12, 1978.
17. CACIF, the Coordinating Committee of Agricultural, Commercial, Industrial and Financial Associations, represents Guatemala's private sector elite.
18. A fellow labour lawyer.
19. Enrique.
20. During the Argentine military's "dirty war" (1976–1983), *las locas de la Plaza de Mayo* — "the madwomen of May Square" — demonstrated most Thursdays in the Plaza de Mayo. Including mothers and grandmothers from all walks of life, the women came together to demand the reappearance *con vida* — "alive" — of family members who had disappeared. Whole families were abducted and the children "adopted" by other families, often in the military. Following the end of the dictatorship, the women pressed for the return of their stolen grandchildren, using DNA typing as the basis for proving kinship. Although they have been successful in recovering some of the lost grandchildren, justice has not been done. Some thirty thousand Argentines went missing in the "dirty war."

21. Marta Gloria Torres' fourth daughter.
22. Oliverio Castañeda de León, president of the University Students' Association, was first on the death list Marta Torres describes. He was killed October 20, 1978.
23. Fellow CNT lawyer Yolanda Urízar.
24. Yolanda Urízar's husband and son were killed in 1975, during an attempt made on her life.
25. As in other parts of the world, Guatemala is now facing a severe ecological crisis. The El Petén rainforest has been classified as the fifth lung of the world, but if severe deforestation continues at the current rate, the forest will be gone in twenty-five years. Chemical spraying has occurred in all Guatemala with concentration in the Pacific coast agricultural zone, where women have been found to have up to 185 times the level of DDT in their breastmilk considered safe by the World Health Organization. Recently it has been revealed that unwanted chemical waste from industrialized countries has been smuggled into Guatemala and dumped in several sites. The grass roots movement is beginning to mobilize around environmental issues. See *La Hora, La muerte química envuelve a los guntemaltecos*, April 5, 1990, p. 52
26. In April 1991, UITA took a further step in consolidating its union work when FESTRAS, the Federation of Food and Allied Workers' Unions, was formed.

In memory of Alaide Foppa —

*After the 1954 coup, feminist intellectual and poet
Alaide Foppa went into exile in Mexico,
accompanied by her husband. While in Mexico, she
co-founded the feminist magazine* fem. *In December
1980, sixty-five-year-old Foppa returned to
Guatemala to visit her ailing mother. She was
kidnapped and is still missing.*

CHAPTER FIVE

Women in Women's Organizations

Women coming together in their own groups is a new expression of grassroots organizing in Guatemala. Traditionally, there have been associations of lawyers' wives and university professors' wives and women's groups in the wealthier parishes performing charitable acts for the needy.[1] However, none of these organizations explored the relationship between women and men. Nor did they seek to challenge the power of the dominant elites.

During the Ten Years of Spring the Guatemalan Women's Alliance brought together progressive women, mostly from the urban middle and upper-middle classes. These women had a sincere interest in bettering the position of women in society and, among other things, started a credit cooperative for campesinas.[2]

After the 1954 coup, women leaders in the grassroots movement faced the same harsh treatment as their male counterparts. The Alliance disappeared. During the next twenty years very few women's organizations formed. A woman's committee emerged in the university students' association. And the Dolores Bedoya de Molina Group spoke out against the violence of the military regime of Peralta Azurdia.[3]

The Women's Solidarity in Action Committee formed in

1975, and the National Women's Union of Guatemala (UNAMG) organized in 1980. Both were short-lived. Following the 1976 earthquake, the Women's Solidarity in Action Committee began to work with women in the areas most hard hit. From 1977 to 1979, the group was in contact with women in the slums, campesinas, women teachers, students, intellectuals and women in the health and service sectors. Out of these discussions came consensus on the need for a broad-based women's organization.

On March 9, 1980, in the midst of some the fiercest oppression ever seen in Guatemala, UNAMG was born. One hundred and twenty *ladinas* and eighty Indigenous women had taken part in the Encounter of Guatemalan Women that led to UNAMG. But many of UNAMG's leaders would be killed or go missing, including Silvia Galvez, the group's primary leader inside Guatemala. The army is thought to be responsible for her disappearance in December 1985. UNAMG continues its work in exile.

In 1986 women began organizing again. That year the Women's Group for the Betterment of the Family (GRUFE-PROMEFAM) formed, first to bring together the wives of unionists. It then expanded and now draws mostly women trade unionists. The Women's Committee of the International Union of Food and Allied Workers' Associations (COMFUITAG) is another union women's group. Both groups are meeting success in educating trade unionists on the importance of women's participation in the labour movement. Both also offer much needed support for the strengthening of women's roles within their unions.

Grupo Tierra Viva and Grupo Guatemalteco de Mujeres are two small feminist groups that have come together over the past few years. They have played a critical role in bringing the structural roots of women's oppression to the discussion table. They have also been active in the Hemispheric Encounters on feminist issues.

The largest women's group to form in recent years is the Guatemalan Widows' National Coordinating Group (CON-AVIGUA). Eight thousand women, mostly Indigenous women widowed by the repression, have come together from all over Guatemala. Their demands include respect for their dignity as women and respect for human rights. They have been a powerful mobilizing force, reaching the most isolated communities. They also work, not without considerable danger, in the zones in conflict.

Indigenous women have traditionally been the most marginalized group in Guatemalan society.

Because of the repression, tens of thousands of Guatemalans have fled the country. And women are organizing in exile as well. In Mexico City several Guatemalan women's groups have come together in NAN, or "mother" in Quiché. NAN includes the UNAMG and Nuestra Voz,[4] a group which also has organized in Canada. Nuestra Voz aims to contribute to changing social structures for the well-being of all Guatemalans and to put an end to the exploitation and oppression of Guatemalan women.

The Mamá Maquín Organization of Refugee Women was formed in May 1990 among women at the refugee camps in the south of Mexico. Mamá Maquín promotes refugee women's right to organize, to educate themselves and to participate on equal terms with men. The group also defends the right to preserve and develop Indigenous cultures and traditions. La Nueva Union (the New Union) is another organization of refugee women in the state of Campeche in southern Mexico.

In August 1989, women from five Central American countries met and formed the Permanent Assembly of Central American Women for Peace. In order to represent Guatemala at this and other meetings, Guatemalan women formed the National Coordinating Committee of Guatemalan Women's Groups. Although this was a positive move, it is somewhat limited by its lack of representation from rural women's groups.

Women organizing in Guatemala are challenging the traditional grassroots political movement to examine itself and its own structures. Their work is extremely difficult. They face obstacles at home, on the street and in the workplace. But the women interviewed say their greatest enemy is the enemy facing all Guatemalans working for change: the small but powerful ruling elite that controls Guatemala economically, politically and militarily.

Violence continues to stalk women organizers. On April 29, 1991, Dinora Pérez, a Social Democratic Party candidate in the 1990 elections, union organizer and founder of the women's group, the María Chinchilla Institute, was machine-gunned to death as she left her car to enter her home.

You Can't Trade a Husband's Love for a Few Pounds of Corn

Rosalina Tuyuc,
Co-ordinator, Board of
Directors, Guatemalan Widows'
National Coordinating Group
(CONAVIGUA)

My name is Rosalina Tuyuc. I'm from Chimaltenango; my language is Cakchiquel. I'm a widow and I have two children.

The violence in our town began in 1980. Day by day, burned, tortured bodies appeared. First they picked up the leaders of each group. They took away catechists, leaders of Indigenous organizations, members of Alcoholics Anonymous, Protestants, pastors of evangelical churches. They took everyone. Some reappeared. Others never did.

I belonged to a group of young people. We began to hear the army was around, looking for leaders. We had to leave, to hide and work in other areas, but our calling has always been to work with our people. At the time, we were rebuilding our town — when the earthquake happened, all the houses had crumbled.

When I left, my whole family stayed in town. But when the army was looking for us — it wasn't just armed groups, but the army itself, driving their jeeps. One day, they entered our home. Since they couldn't find us — three of us were working with the youth group; the work was mostly praying, saying the rosary, discussing the Bible — they took my father. He was fifty-four years old, and he worked making rosaries for the Church. He led a choir in the parish. They took him away. And to this day, we don't know anything. My mother was traumatized because of his disappearance. In addition to this, the soldiers came back to look for us. Our house was under a lot of surveillance.

But we knew we hadn't done anything. Our work was out in the open. The community knew us well. Our only crime was that we knew who was doing the killing. Our people can't speak Spanish, let alone read or write it. The women never get to study. Women are always valued less than men. But we know we have the same rights.

One day my husband went out to work and never came back. He's been missing since May 24, 1985. The last information I got was that they were holding him at the military base in Chimaltenango. About two years ago, I heard he was alive. I couldn't lay charges with any authorities — I knew about thousands who'd met with the same fate. Nobody finds out anything. And even if you lay charges, they never do anything.

Three months after he disappeared, men in plainclothes came to the house asking for him. They said he was alive, and that he was at the military base in Zacapa, and that he wanted to talk to me. I told them that I hadn't heard anything from him. I didn't go with them because I knew they were lying. That's how I was widowed, left with my children. They're five and six years old now.

They're always asking when he's going to come back. I tell them he's far away from us but always thinking of them. As a mother, it hurts to tell them he's never coming back. You're always hoping maybe he'll come home. It's been so long since he has been here. The little girl was a year old when she was left with me. The boy was two years and two months and he remembers a lot about his father. He loved him very much. At least I know his work was helping our people work and live in dignity.

Bringing up the little ones has been very difficult for me. It was the rainy season when he disappeared, and I walked with my girl on my back, carrying the other one, with their clothes in my other hand.

I looked for him in the detention centres, the jails. And I thought maybe there'd been an accident. I looked for him through the fire department and in the hospitals. But nobody told me anything. A lot of bodies were turning up back then. Almost always I bought a newspaper, or listened to the news, but there was nothing.

The pain is so great you can't measure it. And more than anything, I depended on God. There wasn't anybody I could talk to about what was going on. Only my heart knew. The neighbours asked me what had happened to him. I said he'd gone off with another woman! But in my heart I felt this ache because I couldn't tell people what had happened. Only a few friends knew.

For two years I couldn't even go out on the street. A month after my husband disappeared — a friend of my husband's had been going everywhere with me, looking. The *judiciales* stopped us on the road one day. They grabbed him and I watched when they took my husband's friend away. They grabbed me too, but maybe luck was with me that day — I was with the two children. They just took him and left me. But when I saw how they grabbed him, I began to think: that's how it happened with my husband. And I wondered where he was. This friend was in the car, tied up, crying.

I knew that GAM was struggling, but I couldn't stand going

out. I couldn't even look at tall men with dark glasses, or at armoured cars. I just couldn't. It was two years before I could see people again. I went out but never very far from where we were living. I couldn't bear going to the centre of town. The children were always saying, "We're hungry." I'd get mad at them, and I wouldn't feed them. I didn't even remember there were mealtimes.

Night would come and I'd feel that ache. But because of the need to eat I finally reacted. I knew there were many other widows who couldn't even talk. We began to get to know each other.

Because of my need to begin again, I began to meet other compañeras exchanging experiences with other women in small communities. We know they've robbed us of our husbands' love. And now they're using the widows. We know we have dignity, have value as women, but they use us in their propaganda. It's just propaganda that they're helping the widows. Only great sacrifices have kept us and our children alive.

I'm the coordinator of the board of directors of CONAVIGUA. We know the only solution is to be united. Nobody knows the exact number of widows, but about forty-five thousand widows have protested the disappearances or kidnappings of their husbands. But there are thousands of cases where only the woman knows what's happened, and she hasn't said anything to the authorities or the neighbours.

About eight thousand widows have joined CONAVIGUA, those who belong to committees. But thousands more have told us they can't join because they've gotten threats from the authorities and the Civil Patrol leaders. We have several cases where leaders have suffered threats and persecution, and a compañera from the board of directors was threatened.[5] The local Patrol leaders say we gave the widows the idea of organizing, that the widows don't want to organize. But the widows have stood up on their own and joined CONAVIGUA.

In Zacualpa, El Quiché, the mayor called all the widows together to receive a little bit of food. But when they came to town, the mayor chose two or three representatives from each community, and he gave it to them. So because the rest were making demands, two were jailed. Five widows were beaten.

After the mass killing at El Aguacate,[6] they forced the widows off their land. Our custom is to cultivate the land, to keep animals, but these compañeras don't have a chance to plant or keep animals. What they have given them is a house. But you can't trade a husband's love for a few pounds of corn or a house. We can't speak with the widows of Aguacate. The military won't let anyone talk to them.

This is just another sign that it's not like the government says in Guatemala — that there's peace, there's democracy, there's calm. That's what's said at the international level, but there's no calm. There's a lot of fear. The military has even told communities there will be more mass killings if they continue to organize. People are afraid because the authorities — military or civilian — don't just say it: they do it.

For the government, development means giving away a little corn, beans and rice. This isn't development, and getting corn and beans every three or four months doesn't get rid of hunger.

We want our people to have access to education, access to medicine. You can't buy medicine these days. Many children are dying just from fevers or diarrhea because our people can't even buy something for that.

There will be development in Guatemala the day women participate and have access to education. Last year the government said it taught one million Guatemalans to read and write. If this is true, then women could read and write, at least write their names. This hasn't happened. The women go to literacy classes because they give them corn.[7] Our people do want to learn, but our compañeras can no longer think about studying; they have to think about how to feed their children, how to educate them.

When people from other countries come to Guatemala, they only go to the lakes, to the tourist areas. They talk a lot about Guatemala because of the ruins. The work of the Mayas may be finished, but we're their descendants. We wear the dress, speak the language. We aren't the past but the present. We'd like people to know how Indigenous people live. Indigenous people in my country haven't been given the place that they deserve. We aren't participating and we are the vast majority.

We're Demanding Our Rights, Our Dignity as Women

María Morales Jorge,
Guatemalan Widows' National
Coordinating Group (CONAVIGUA)

My name is María Morales Jorge. I'm from Chichicastenango, in El Quiché. I'm single and I'm working with widows. Our organization calls on all women who want to participate — widows, single women, young women. That's how I became a member of the national board of directors.

I was working in Chichicastenango parish. We had a radio program, "Catholic Voice." Every Thursday we had a broadcast for widows and women in general. That's when the widows came to explain their problems. It hurt me a lot when I realized we weren't going to get anywhere with preaching. So I spoke with a priest, Father Ventura Lush Herrera, who was working in Chichicastenango. I told him about the need for a widows' group, with its own leadership, so they could begin to look after their own needs. The way it was, they were crying all the time and we were just sending special greetings to them on Thursdays. It didn't do anything for them, just made them sadder.

So he agreed and we sat down to think about the best way to bring the widows together. Now that May was coming, we decided to take advantage of the Day of the Virgin and call them to a mass on May 14, 1988. We invited all the widows from Chichicastenango, and we hoped widows from other towns would come too. The day of the mass, widows from nine municipalities showed up! About two thousand widows had come together. The church was filled. They'd never had a chance to talk about the pain they'd suffered so the mass was a release for them.

Two weeks later, Patrol leaders in Chichicastenango got together and said the priest was subversive and part of GAM. The mass was celebrated on May 14th; on June 27th the army had him thrown out of the parish.

The army spoke with Patrol leaders and the leaders forced people to demonstrate against the priest. Once they'd gotten rid of the priest, they began to ridicule the widows, saying they were all over the place because they didn't have husbands. "If we don't kill them right away, we're going to divide them up. Each man will get seven widows" — that's what they said.

So the widows felt desperate. And they had other serious problems. Other people said it was their fault the priest wasn't there. In the end they didn't know where to go — there were threats from all sides. It was very painful, but I couldn't leave them. Other young women got discouraged, but I told them that wasn't any good. We couldn't lose heart.

That's when the widows' group began. Before they had committees, but they hadn't set up a municipal or departmental executive. So we did that. Even though there are problems, we're bringing widows together so they won't lose heart. They're very brave. When people realized the women were beginning to unite, some looked for ways to destroy their unity.

I didn't know what to do. The work was important, but the Church was afraid to help us because they'd gotten rid of Father Ventura. Nobody with any authority looked out for us. But the widows got more involved. Widows came from Sololá. We didn't know what to do about what they were saying about us. They began to talk about me, saying, "This woman isn't even a widow. Why doesn't she get married?" There wasn't much support.

Then the widows from Chimaltenango came to us in July and August. In September, we decided to form the National Coordinating Group. I didn't want to be on the board of directors. I'm not a widow. But they wanted me to be a spokeswoman for them. Now that we have the board of directors, the work is coordinated. Almost every compañera has her area of work, and by living with people, she gets to know about their situations.

Because we haven't had a chance to study or work, women have been in a rut for a very long time. We're demanding our rights, our dignity as women. As persons. We want education for the children. As well, we want those responsible for the assassinations punished. Those are our demands.

We Gain Courage from Other Women

*The Women's Group for the
Betterment of the Family
(GRUFEPROMEFAM)*

Our first idea was to organize the wives of union leaders. We thought that by helping the women they would better understand the role their compañeros were playing in the unions and that this would strengthen the work. But this would have been very limited. And most of us were single mothers. We had to change our goals and our work plan, to create a plan that would bring us closer to the grassroots movement.

We thought our group should be broader, involving women from different sectors: working-class compañeras, homemakers, teachers, wives of union leaders. When we broadened our group, we found our emphasis needed to be more on working-class women, on compañeras who work in the unions. Right now our group works mostly with working-class women.

Our group was born in 1986. We're called the Women's Group for the Betterment of the Family: GRUFEPROMEFAM. We believe the family is part of the fabric of society and women are a vital part of society.

In our environment it's very difficult to work with women. We were raised to be at home, to serve a husband and the children. That's how they brought us up, and it's very difficult to get a compañera to come out and participate. In 1987 we opened up spaces, building the foundations of our group. In 1988 we undertook broader work.

When we began there wasn't any analysis of women's situation. At first we didn't have an analysis because that wasn't our goal at the time. But as women from different sectors began to participate, this became very important for us. Each sector's contributions, with its own characteristics, gave us new factors we had to consider.

We had to set up a plan the compañeros would understand and help to carry out, because at first their machismo and other values made them see this as a struggle against men. We had to show in our work that this wasn't our goal.

We began with talks based on the compañeras understanding, capabilities and interests. We also held activities to strengthen our connection with the union movement in particular. We held fund-raising events to help Lunafil, Acumuladores Víctor, the Bakery Workers, and later Transcontinental and Petrosteel.[8] Our gatherings had two goals: to bring union families together and to turn the proceeds over to those same people.

We had a family cultural Sunday outside the factory with the families of the compañeros who'd occupied Lunafil. What was most important was those compañeros saw the support they were getting from their families and from compañeros from other unions.

At Christmastime Petrosteel had problems. Along with UNSITRAGUA and UITA, we had a Christmas celebration for the compañeros' children. It might seem like the workers' movement has only one demand, but each sector has its own demands. We came to understand the daily lives and working lives of these women.

We promote human rights and the struggle for peace. We held a conference about peace in Central America, something very important considering the situation in Central America, particularly in Guatemala.

We've gotten to know some Protestant campesinas. They told us they no longer wanted to clean the church, change the flowers and take collections — they had other needs. They said the pastor had always told them to respect and obey their compañeros.

In January 1989 we held the First Encounter of Working Women. The goals of the meeting were to open up space for discussing working-class women's problems and to set our goals. Through the participation of the women in the group and their different experiences we established our platform.

In 1988 we took part in a workshop on the rights of women workers, in Mexico. We also took part in activities held by two women's organizations in El Salvador. That was very interesting for us because we learned new ways of working.

Although we have more than two hundred members, not all take part in our meetings. One reason is that women have always been in charge of the children. We have to arrange child care so the mothers can come to meetings. This is one reason we haven't gotten very far in our work. Nonetheless, the women are very important in the grassroots movement. A decade ago, there were no women's organizations in the grassroots movement.

The repression dividing our country has been fierce. We don't know what's going to happen. At any time our organizations could be eliminated. As women, we can't do anything from the outside to protest these waves of repression. But we can do something from within the unions. And even if organizations are eliminated, they carry on with new types of work.

Promoting the rights of women is a very big task; it's going to take a long time, but it had to begin somewhere. It's important we know the civil code, the labour code, the constitution and the unions' collective agreements. The workshops we hold to help to meet this goal include "Women and Work," "Women and the Union," "Women and Peace" and "Women and the Law."

As an organization, we celebrate International Women's Day. Because of its origins, we value this day a lot. We make it a day of commemoration and reflection.

There are no barriers to solidarity between the women of GRUFEPROMEFAM and the women of the world. Thanks to solidarity, we've managed to carry out our work. It's not easy, but it's not impossible. We gain courage from other women. And we know we face similar consequences because of the systems that govern us. We send our solidarity and strength to the women of the world.

We Can't Isolate Ourselves

Tierra Viva
Women's Group

If we were to locate the roots of Tierra Viva, they would be in feminist meetings in Mexico in November 1986. It was there we participated in this kind of feminism for the first time. We presented a position paper that was purely political, without realizing at the time that feminism was political. The Chilean women in these meetings asked us why we didn't have women's groups. They'd managed to set up more than a hundred groups in the midst of the dictatorship. At these meetings, we heard for the first time that feminism wasn't something that happened outside the struggle. We even met people who'd been active in solidarity work and who were very aware of the situation in Central America.

After this, there was real support for us. As a lead-in to the Fourth Feminist Encounter, we brought together one Salvadorean, one Honduran and one Guatemalan woman. We prepared a workshop on the Central American woman. We wanted to present issues from our perspective, and for the first time we managed to have seventeen Guatemalan representatives: trade unionists, teachers, Indigenous women, women who couldn't read or write. We were like a puzzle, with many pieces.

During this meeting the question, "why don't we do something specifically on women?" came up. Although many of the women who participated didn't continue these activities, two of us are here in Tierra Viva. When we went back to our country, we began to have meetings. Other women also began to participate.

We began with reflections about our situation as women, about our specific problems and how we could find solutions for them. The goal we identified was to build ourselves to a level where we could provide stronger support within the grassroots movement. We thought concrete actions within the grassroots movement would give us a chance to develop ourselves.

The group is called Tierra Viva because we believe women not only give life when they have a child but give life wherever they go.

In January 1988 when we first came together, there were eleven of us. We defined our initial goal as consolidating the group and getting in contact with other women's groups.

A project we're setting up is a women's centre, with three areas. One is health, preventive mother-child care. We would do pre- and post-natal care. As well, there will be emotional support for one year after the child is born.

The other area would be law. Up until now, there's been an information vacuum about the requirements for marriage or divorce, on why it's important legally for children to be recognized by the father, on the countless cases of rape.

We can't deny there's political violence directed against activists in Guatemala. But we also can't deny there's domestic violence, a result of the same society. There are women who are very active in the grassroots movement who don't have anyone to talk with about domestic violence because of the great prejudice there is against feminism — that it will take strength away from the movement.

We believe it's completely the opposite because to the extent that women are aware and well-trained for participation in the movement, they're going to be very important in supporting the struggle in Guatemala.

The third area, where we're most advanced, is documentation. We began to pull together material, with the idea that the public would have access to it.

Our key point is that we try to integrate sex, race and class. To have it written down is very easy, but to carry it out in practice is much more difficult. We have begun a series of workshops, some for our own development and others with other women.

Before it was very common in the movement to invite someone to come and give us an analysis about what we wanted. But then we began to analyze the situation in our country. We asked ourselves how we saw the situation, as women.

As women, we've become aware that our work is necessary. We can't isolate ourselves or allow problems to isolate us. We want to find better solutions to the problems. Our group is a feminist group, based on Guatemalan reality. We believe we have to search for our own space. Our group is self-financed and many of us are living in poverty. But we're making this project happen. And our group comes out of our own experiences, our own limitations. It's for us.

When they hear we're working in the feminist movement, they say we're screwing up the work. But the six of us who make up the group are convinced of the importance of our work and of what we are achieving. We're giving our time, but this work is for us.

Endnotes

1. National Women's Office, 1991.
2. UNAMG, *Apuntes para la historia de la Unión Nacional de Mujeres Guatemaltecas* (Mexico City: UNAMG, undated), p. 1.
3. Ibid., p. 2.
4. Nuestra Voz: Our Voice.
5. CONAVIGUA member María Mejía was killed in 1990.
6. In November 1988, the bodies of twenty-two campesinos were discovered in El Aguacate, Chimaltenango. The Guatemalan government immediately accused the guerrillas, but that claim was later discounted by national and international human rights groups.
7. The Guatemalan Committee for Justice and Peace notes that literacy classes have been used to try to separate Indigenous peoples, particularly children, from their language and culture. See Handy, *Gift of the Devil*, p. 260.
8. Important labour struggles of the late-1980s.

In memory of Rogelia Cruz and Nora Paiz —

Rogelia Cruz and Nora Paiz were two of the first women combatants in the Rebel Armed Forces (FAR). Rogelia Cruz was Miss Guatemala in 1959. Cruz and Paiz were killed by the military in 1967.

CHAPTER SIX

Women in Arms

When the Guatemalan people found all non-violent paths to change blocked off by a rigid elite, bent on holding onto power at any cost, they took up arms. "This is a war we're being forced to fight. It's not that we like war, it's not because we're warriors. Rather, it's a necessity if we are to obtain a real democracy in Guatemala."[1]

The roots of Guatemala's modern insurgents lie in the Conquest. The current expression began in the early 1960s. A failed coup on November 13, 1960 involved a third of the Guatemalan Army. It was led by young military officers and sowed the seeds for the revolutionary movement fighting today. In 1962 the Rebel Armed Forces (FAR) was born. The FAR began to organize in eastern Guatemala and by 1966 enjoyed some grassroots support. Using the *foco* as its model, the FAR set up small armed groups which were meant to ignite the entire country into rebellion.

That same year, government counterinsurgency campaigns began, with advisers from a seriously concerned United States government. Between 1966 and 1968, Guatemalan security forces murdered thousands of campesinos who were suspected to be supporters of the insurgents. The guerrilla organization was severely weakened. After armed resistance failed in the sixties, surviving members of the guerrilla forces retreated, regrouped, analyzed the country and their own organizations and then slowly began to reassert themselves. The FAR moved into the capital and began to organize within the grassroots movement. In 1978 the FAR opened fronts in Guatemala City, El Petén and Chimaltenango.

After years of quiet organizing, two new revolutionary organizations went public: the Guerrilla Army of the Poor (EGP), and the Revolutionary Organization of the People in Arms (ORPA). The EGP drew its strength from the central Highlands, in El Quiché, Huehuetenango, Alta Verapaz, Baja Verapaz and Chimaltenango. ORPA organized in the western and central Highlands and on the south coast in San Marcos, Quetzaltenango, Sololá, Totonicapán and Huehuetenango.

By the early 1980s, revolutionary organizations were active in nineteen of Guatemala's twenty-two departments. In 1982 the three organizations came together with a fourth group, the leadership core of the Guatemalan Labour Party (PGT), to create an umbrella group, the Guatemalan National Revolutionary Unity (URNG).

For the past thirty years Guatemalan governments, both military and civilian, have launched successive counterinsurgency campaigns. Unable to put an end to the guerrillas, the army targets the civilian population. The results for the Guatemalan people, as many of the women's narratives express, have been devastating. Nonetheless, the armed resistance has remained a constant force, and the conditions which sparked its creation are ever more desperate.

The government had hoped the revolutionary movement would disintegrate with the breakup of Eastern Europe and the defeat of the Sandinistas in Nicaragua's 1990 elections. The revolutionaries themselves have said all along that their struggle was a national one.

By 1991, guerrillas were again operating in fourteen departments, including the capital, which had been without guerrilla activity since 1980. They have also taken the diplomatic offensive: a rebel-initiated round of talks began in 1990. These negotiations have included many sectors of Guatemalan society and are aimed at building a national consensus towards finding a peaceful resolution to the three decades of armed conflict.

Within the revolutionary movement, women's issues are only now being seriously considered, despite the fact that women had been involved in the guerrilla movement of the 1960s. But it appears the male insurgents of the time found their own views on women confirmed by the well-respected Latin American revolutionary Ernesto "Che" Guevara. Although Guevara acknowledged that women can fight, he also offered this view of women's role in the struggle:

> But also at this stage (in the revolutionary war) a woman can perform her habitual tasks of peacetime; it is very pleasing to a soldier subjected to the extremely hard conditions of this life to be able to look forward to a seasoned meal which tastes like something. The woman as cook can greatly improve diet and furthermore, it is easier to keep her in these domestic tasks; one of the problems in guerrilla bands is that all works of a civilian character are scorned by those who perform them; they are constantly trying to get out of these tasks in order to enter into forces that are actively in combat.[2]

But as cooks or as combatants, women *were* part of the insurgency of the sixties. And many of them were killed. Nora Paiz was killed in March 1967. Coming down from the eastern mountains, she was captured with Guatemalan revolutionary poet, Otto René Castillo. They were held and tortured for four days and then burned alive. Rogelia Cruz, Miss Guatemala of 1959, was killed in 1967. Clemencia Paiz, Fantina Rodríguez Padilla, Michelle Firk of France, Iris Yon Cerna and Eunice Campiran de Aguilar Mora of Mexico also died in the revolutionary struggle of the 1960s.

Beginning in the sixties, women have also become leaders at most levels in revolutionary organizations. Still, the end of women's oppression has yet to be accepted as an integral part of the struggle for social justice. The "women's question" is not high on the list of priorities and when women advance it is only as individuals within the organizations. The need for the full participation and advancement of women within the revolutionary movement is yet to be faced. The situation of Guatemala's Indigenous peoples merited full attention in the URNG's Unity Proclamation in 1982; but the status of women was mentioned only as a sub-point under the general theme of creating a new society: "Women will have the same rights as men, since they share the same obligations as men, and even greater ones in their role as mothers."[3]

Past national liberation struggles have assumed that with the seizing of power by the revolutionary forces, the source of women's oppression will vanish. But many women and men within the Guatemalan revolutionary movement are coming to realize that the success of a national liberation struggle does not in itself guarantee the end of women's oppression. For the first time, the concept that women's oppression has its roots in something lying beyond the economic structure is appearing in revolutionary thought. And it is becoming clear to the movement that the struggle to transform society must itself be transformed and broadened. Guatemalan women are demanding it be broadened now.

We Are Not Going to Face
Guns with Just Our Voices

Catalina, URNG

I consider myself to have been very fortunate in my childhood and youth because I happened to have been born into a very happy home, with access to comfort, to schooling and much more. But I could see that while I lived like that injustices were close by.

We lived in the capital during the school year, and for vacations we went to the country. I remember the conditions of rural workers, especially the Indigenous people. They lived in big sheds, like chicken coops. Every year, they would make a new cemetery for children who had died.

Once when I was riding a horse, I saw a woman and two men go by carrying some poles, with a package wrapped up in newspaper on top. The woman was crying, and I asked her what was wrong. She didn't answer, just stared at me with a look I'll never forget: a look of hatred. Then the man said, "Excuse her. Her child died and we're going to bury him." I was just a girl, maybe eight years old or younger.

I saw how workers were treated by my family and friends, and it seemed very unjust. I played with their daughters. We were happy and we absolutely never did anything wrong. But when I got home, they'd beat me for keeping bad company.

When I was only three or four, I noticed on the plantations they'd beat the workers for some infraction. They kept them shackled in a small room for several days, on nothing but bread and water. Once a woman from one the wealthiest families of Guatemala put her servant in a goose pond to punish her for not having set the table properly. When the servant was drowning she had her taken out and then put in again. Then she went calmly off to eat.

I was educated by nuns in a Catholic school, and I asked the nuns, if God is just, why were there rich and poor? They told me, "It is easier for a camel to pass through the eye of a needle than for a rich man to enter the Kingdom of Heaven." Later, they said if you repented at the last minute you'd go to heaven. To my way of thinking, it didn't matter what you did in your life.

This mix — the luxury, my religious upbringing and reality — turned me around. I think I joined the armed struggle for emotional reasons, not out of clarity or conviction. I had all this accumulated experience, but I didn't have it processed. You naturally lean more towards comfort.

So I lived like that; I let myself be swallowed up by the environment until one of my brothers joined. He told me from the very beginning he was joining, and he asked me to help him. At the time, I already knew there were guerrillas, fighting for the poor. They'd already aroused my sympathy. I loved him very much, and I told him he could count on me for whatever he wanted.

Around that time they killed Rogelia Cruz. I hadn't known she was a guerrilla, and we'd been friends. It affected me deeply. Once we were eating at the home of a wealthy man, and his daughter said to him, "But look Papa, how could they do that?" And he replied, "She was asking for it. There's one law here: guerrilla seen, guerrilla dead." At the time, I was already working with the guerrillas.

Rogelia's death moved even the most immovable. But I noticed it wasn't like that for these people: nothing mattered beyond their own immediate interests. How is that possible?

I told myself: These people are in church every Sunday; they have everything and can do everything. How come they aren't moved by something so obvious?

Those were the first steps. Two years later, I met the man who now is my compañero. I'm married and now I have four children. I could say I have grandchildren because I'm raising a new generation, not directly, but indirectly. If they are well-educated, children and young people are our guarantee for the future.

When you're convinced and you're aware, nothing can interfere. I've told my children a revolutionary can't have schedules. I'm there twenty-four hours — I wish there were more hours in the day; what we have isn't enough. I've done almost everything — you do what needs to be done and learn what needs to be learned.

I remember my father had guns in the house. When he had them out, I wouldn't go near them because people had told me guns were the devil's work. I was horrified by the weapons. I had to learn to use them and I did.

For women, becoming part of the revolution has been a struggle, an assertion of our rights. We've had to move forward, fighting for — and winning — the right to participate. For example, when I joined, the only tasks assigned to us were stakeouts, providing security for a compañero preparing for an operation, preparing meals while the compañeros worked, cleaning house — those kinds of jobs.

We never accepted that. We rebelled and began to demand other kinds of responsibilities and the compañeros really let loose on us. They accused us of being comfortable and petit bourgeois, of not valuing domestic work — this was coming from our own compañeros!

When I came into a collective — I was the only woman for a long time — everything was a disaster. The food was poorly prepared, the house in shambles, stuff thrown here and there. The first day I cleaned, organized, cooked and served with great enthusiasm. And while I was doing this, the others were studying, preparing and reading. The second day, I did it again, but then I saw they were going on as before. The third day, I got up and I posted a list dividing up the tasks, and I went to read and study. They really came down on top of me, but I didn't budge. I didn't fix any meals and I devoted myself to reading. From then on — despite attacks and long faces — my compañeros were forced to accept it.

That was my first victory. I said, "In my house, they served me. I didn't come here to serve, I came to do my part. But for it to work out, everyone needs to contribute. We can organize it among ourselves. I'm not prepared to do your work anymore because what time am I going to have?"

The collective began to change. Other compañeras in other collectives were doing the same and we began to show what we could do.

Another stage began with the intensifying of the armed struggle. In the beginning there was a tendency for compañeras to be given certain tasks, while the compañeros went to fight — until there were compañeras who proved themselves and rebelled against that. In combat, they were sometimes braver than the men.

Then women combatants began to gain the respect of the compañeros, but they had to prove themselves in practice to be recognized the way they are today. In the past, there were very few women; we all knew one another. Now there are a lot of compañeras in all areas of the revolutionary movement, in all organizations, in all areas of work.

Rogelia and Nora were among the first. There were others, such as Miriam and Antonieta. Miriam was seventeen years old and eight-and-a-half-months pregnant when she was horribly killed. They captured her, kicked her and forced her into labour. They killed her child to make her talk, and then they burned Miriam alive. Antonieta was also pregnant when they killed her.

Although I knew them both, I was closer to Miriam. I got to know her as a person, her moral qualities, her courage, the decisiveness she showed until the end. If she had wanted to, she could have done us a lot of damage at that time. We were in a state of flux, our resources were very limited, and she knew a lot about that.

Sometimes, before she was killed, I would get depressed because my compañero wasn't around. But she always pushed me on. Miriam was the person who most encouraged me to go the limit — I still don't know if I'm going to die in this. Even though she was younger than me, she had great firmness of purpose.

For me and for many other compañeras, whenever we find ourselves in a tight spot — when we're running a big risk or about to be captured — we immediately think of these women. That's where we get more strength because we feel a big commitment to these compañeras. They are an example for the rest of us. After death they continue to play a role. They continue to contribute to the struggle because we really never will forget them. When we say, "So and so ... *presente!*" they are with us. They're part of that steel rod you sometimes have to use to keep strong.

At first you keep going because you've thought about the situation and because you understand the problem from a theoretical point of view — because you've become aware, made a decision. But this isn't enough sometimes. You need feelings and ethics to keep you going. You have to nourish this. And it can't be done with books, it can't be done with words. That's why we say the blood of the fallen has nourished the struggle. Their example is like a sprinkling of water on a flower — it helps us carry on.

When you're in the mountains and you're tired and think you can't take another step, you begin to remember your compañeros. You begin to think about the people. You begin to think about your commitment to those who have fallen, your commitment to those walking beside you. Then you realize you've been walking for another five hours, on commitment alone. It's not energy — the body doesn't respond anymore. On the march you're thinking about the mass killings, people's suffering. And before you know it, you've already done what you thought was impossible.

This is a very difficult time for all humanity, and I think the conditions exist for women's participation on a wide scale, at the global level. We all share an urgent need for peace. The whole world needs peace. Women are ready and they're going to play an enormous role.

It isn't the same for men in the struggle for peace and for democracy. There is a difference. For example, in Guatemala there are thousands and thousands of widows. And the women who've lost their children — this is something you can never recover from. That is the worst that can happen to a mother. I'm not saying it isn't terrible for men, but they've spent less time with their children. The mothers feel their absence more, those restless nights.

When we were working in the city, nights were spent waiting. You say to yourself: "If they come to the house, what am I going to do with the babies? If they find them, they're going to torture them, and I won't be able to take it. Or, I can take it. I won't speak, but death would be preferable to seeing my child tortured in front of me."

You can't sleep. I think if I talked to women who aren't involved as I am, they'd think the same. Then I'd think: "It would be better if I shot each of my children and then shot myself, so they couldn't take us alive." Then came the contradiction: "They're asleep and they won't notice. But that would be the first one; the others would wake up with the noise."

It's not something tangible, you can't feel it or write it down, there aren't any photos of it. It's the accumulation of the suffering women live with. I can say this because it's something that I've felt in my own flesh, and I've heard it from women who are involved with the struggle and from those who aren't. There are mothers who stay glued to the radios, listening for the discovery of bodies, listening for the names of their children.

Sometimes I don't think about Guatemala because if I begin to think about it, I'll end up crying. It's too much. These are the consequences of the war; these are the consequences of the lack of democracy; these are the consequences of the unrest through all the military governments, and now with civilian government.

It would be hard to find a family in Guatemala that hasn't been affected by this — revolutionaries, reactionaries, or neither. More than a few people have lost a friend, a neighbour, a family member — it is so widespread and so truly collective that any woman in Guatemala could organize around this issue. But there's a lot of fear. We know organizing could cost our lives. And we have commitments to keep, for example, the commitment to raise children who've lost their fathers — the fear of dying and leaving the children orphans. And there's the natural human fear of facing death.

These things aren't known in many places. Because of the lack of democracy, the women in our country are at war. We're struggling to free ourselves, to reach peace and democracy. I don't know of another country like Guatemala, where we're so repressed and where there is so little freedom to struggle for our social and political demands.

We are not going to face guns with just our voices. We're not going to face torturing thugs with words alone. We can't because they are truly beasts.

A compañero told me, "I had no idea what the guerrillas were like, but I'm the only survivor in my family. One night the army came in, and they killed my wife and my children and my nieces and nephews, and I was wounded. They left me for dead. The only thing I could do was go to my cousin's house. My cousin was with a group. I asked him how to find the guerrillas because the army was going to kill me. But I didn't know anything about guerrillas — I knew they were in the mountains, but I'd never taken part in anything. Then my cousin said, 'If you really want to go I'll take you.' So he brought me and here I am."

Once in the western part of the country there was a mass killing. The guerrillas weren't there, but they heard about it. Three days later — two full days had already gone by — the guerrillas arrived and found a pile of bodies. Dogs were eating the bodies. Then they heard a noise, and at first they thought it was a dog, but then they heard a cry. It was a child sucking at his dead mother's breast. He was alive. They picked him up, bathed him and took him with them. We have this boy. He's seven years old now.

What do you think this boy is going to be when he grows up? This boy knows what happened. So what should we expect? What's this child going to do after what they did to his village? It wasn't just his mother and his father and his relatives. Is it going to be enough for him to go to the Congress and complain?

We revolutionaries don't like war. We're fighting for life. And it makes us sad to see how these military men can feel such disdain for life when we're giving everything we have to save it. We really don't understand this bestiality and in-humanity. Sometimes people think that we go out coldly, to kill like they do. No. We go to defend life. Not just our lives, but the lives of children, women, older people, the lives of the people of Guatemala.

I've always been sure of victory. I've always been sure that someday justice will prevail in Guatemala, even if we don't live to see it.

While the Real Power Lies
with the Military, There
Won't Be Any Change

Judith, URNG

My name is Judith. I'm originally from the capital of Guatemala. Both my parents had to work very hard to support us and send us to school. There were only two children, but our situation was very difficult economically. I lived on the edge of a very poor neighbourhood. I knew many people there, how they lived, the problems they had — the same problems that my family had in maintaining us.

Then too, we lived with the repression from the beginning. My father had been a union member at the time of the revolution of 1944 to 1954. And when Castillo Armas[4] came in, they jailed him just for being in a union, accused of being a communist. When they killed Castillo Armas,[5] they jailed him again, for the same reason.

This made a big impression on me, even though I was very young. I'd also met some Cuban compañeros who'd left Cuba after the assault on the Moncada barracks.[6] When some of them were released they came to Guatemala, and my parents helped the Cubans. So I have an image of them, of how they wanted to return to their homeland and fight to liberate it.

I was seventeen years old when I joined a study group, my first step in joining the struggle. I was doing clandestine work, so I didn't get involved in anything at school. Beginning in 1971, I got more directly involved, and in 1972, I became a full-time cadre. A little later, I got involved with a compañero in my organization and we had two daughters. But we separated eleven years ago. I had a son who died, and I was left alone with my two daughters. They're big now.

Ever since my daughters were born — one is four years older than the other — I've had to leave them to be raised by compañeros and compañeras. I couldn't have taken care of them, especially when I was in the mountains. There have been times when we've been in the same country, but not together, not even for a few days. Other times we've lived together, and certainly they understand. Since they were little I've talked to them about the struggle and about why I have to leave them. It hasn't been easy, not for them and not for me.

For me, the revolution comes first. If you can sacrifice yourself, you can also sacrifice your parents and your children. I haven't heard anything from my parents since 1980. I don't know if they're dead or alive. I don't know what's happened to my brother or my nephews. Most of my compañeros are dead.

When you're in Guatemala, living in safe houses, working clandestinely, you wonder when the enemy's going to arrive and what you're going to do. Whether they'll get your children, torture them, rape them if they're girls, so you'll talk. You know you won't live if you're captured. It's very difficult. We don't all take it in the same way, but that's how it's been for me. Many compañeras are in the same situation. It wasn't my personal interests or those of my daughters that came first, but rather the well-being of the entire people. There's no doubt about it.

We've become aware that it's hard for women to join the revolution. To some extent, women can't respond in the same way as men to the necessities of the revolution. On top of our revolutionary role we have our domestic role: the kitchen, the cleaning, the washing, the shopping, the care of our children. It's not like that for men. Even if the compañeros are very aware and very clear, they say the revolution comes first and then the house. But most women can't act that way. You can't tell your children to wait for you to finish something and then you'll nurse them or feed them, or if they're sick, take them to the doctor. There are times you have to set priorities. And on one hand, you're finishing some task, but you're thinking: there's no bread or milk at home.

Many compañeros are taking more of the responsibility at home, but not so long ago they took advantage of their compañeras. They took them along to cook, to wash, to do guard duty, but nothing else. But we've moved ahead and won our space.

We've shown that in spite of having responsibilities at home and having other jobs, we've met our responsibilities in most cases. There are relatively very few of us in comparison to the large number of men who are involved. But up to now, no compañera who has fallen into the hands of the enemy has talked. With women, it's much more difficult for us to join, to dedicate ourselves to the revolution. It's slow work, much slower than for the men. But when we join we're completely committed and ready for anything. It takes more time for a woman to join, but she is stronger, more certain than a man. I don't know of any compañeras who have abandoned the struggle. Some have left the organization because of ideological differences. But even with their differences, they continue within the process.

I can't say exactly how many women there are in the organization. You don't know all the structures. But there are a lot, and many are fighting in the war zones; they're brave fighters, maybe even braver than the men. There's the case of one compañera: one day they were in combat and a compañero wanted to flee from the line of fire. The compañera told him, "Take one step and I'm going to kill you." And the *compa*,[7] he had to stay there until it was over.

There are brave compañeras. I can't compare myself to them. I don't have their ability to walk, to carry a load, to fight. I really admire them. They even give birth there in the jungle — that would be pure death for me — without a doctor, in unsanitary conditions. And pregnant women — carrying loads, doing all sorts of work, as if it was nothing, and then giving birth. There they go carrying their children. During combat they leave them with someone in the village, but they have their children with them.

We are fighting this war for the same reasons that exist throughout the Third World: misery, hunger, malnutrition, no housing, no work. Even minimal organizing isn't permitted in Guatemala. Not even for a wage increase. Not even for better working conditions. It hasn't been allowed since 1954. Not even progressive political parties. In Guatemala, those who fight for better living conditions, for wage increases, for medicine, for health centres, for roads, for schools are, at the very least, threatened with death and have to leave the country. Those who don't are often killed.

The statistics on assassinations, disappearances, mass killings, torture, internal and external refugees are low compared to what has really happened in Guatemala. Sometimes people die at the door of a hospital because there aren't any beds, there's no medicine. Sometimes five-year-old children have to go to work.

Once I was out with my daughter and I sat down beside a

woman who was carrying her daughter. Instead of milk, the bottle had water, and the little girl was crying, asking for milk. The woman told her she'd give her milk when they got home. I felt guilty that I could give my daughter milk when there were people who couldn't even do that.

It's not just in Africa that people die of hunger and malnutrition. In any hospital in Guatemala, in any hamlet, in any town, including in the capital itself — if you go to the poor neighbourhoods — you're going to find children with severe malnutrition. Children die because they have nothing to eat.

That's what's behind the war. In the meantime, the minority can give five pounds of meat to their dogs. Other people can't even afford bread. They go to the garbage dump and get what they can. A whole sector of the population lives off what others have thrown away. The men who work the garbage trucks go through the garbage, and when the truck gets to the dump in Zone Seven, others pick through the garbage to see what goodies are left over. When they dump the garbage, other people are waiting, and they live off what people in the city throw away.

There's no space for open political struggle. Political parties have been outlawed. The FUR (United Front of the Revolution) and the PSD (Democratic Socialist Party) aren't revolutionary parties, but even they can't operate, let alone labour, student and professional leaders — they've been assassinated or threatened with death.

What we have now is a democracy in name only. As long as there's repression, as long as there's no political space, we're going to keep fighting for a real democracy. It's not that we like war, it's not that we're warriors. We want the new Guatemala to be a free country, where there's free expression, where there's work, where there's education, where there's housing, where we have a chance to develop ourselves, to study, to live in peace. That's what we're fighting for.

The URNG is fighting on three fronts: in the north, in the west and southwest, and in central Guatemala. In 1988 we were operating in El Petén, El Quiché, Huehuetenango, San Marcos, Sololá, Chimaltenango, Suchitepéquez and Quetzaltenango. We've broken through the isolation the enemy had forced us into. Now we're operating in eleven departments. A year ago, URNG guerrillas were active in about 50 percent of Guatemala's territory. Now we're in more than that 50 percent, including the capital — which is very important — and Escuintla and Retalhuleu on the coast.[8]

There was a time when we concentrated on hostage taking, on armed propaganda, on occupying roads and villages. Not now. Now we're attacking barracks and army bases. They still call us a "little group of delinquent subversives." But this "little group" has downed airplanes and helicopters, without anti-aircraft weapons. We fight because we're confident we're going to bring change to Guatemala. We're clearer than we used to be, more aware of what we want. We're not going to be satisfied by promises. People are coming to see that the real problem is the army. It doesn't matter which party is in power: while the real power lies with the military, there won't be any change.

A Quick Glimpse of Women's Lives in the Guatemalan Jungle

*Women from
the Rebel Armed Forces (FAR),
a Member Organization
of the Guatemalan National
Revolutionary Unity (URNG)*[9]

The Guatemalan jungle is very green, dark and hostile, with millions of bloodthirsty mosquitoes and insects, and the ever-present deer, wild boars, snakes, lizards, alligators and birds. The light filters through gigantic trees tied together with tangles of vines, lighting up strange pictures on the warm texture of the foliage below. We often search for water in vain. Despite the torrential rains, the earth swallows every drop. Once in a while, in the heart of the jungle, we find beautiful fruits flavoured like divine nectar.

The air is permeated with the aroma of infinite vegetation. Sounds — some musical, others threatening, the cave-dweller screams of howler monkeys and the soft song of the mockingbird — orchestrate storms and shift our emotions from a state of calm to one of alert; the simple pleasure of listening to jungle music, until a rough voice announces in the middle of the night: "It's your turn on guard duty."

There are many women among the Guatemalan insurgents. What are we like? We are short (about five feet tall on average), courageous, hardworking and dressed in olive green. Most combatants were peasants before joining; many of us are Indigenous women and Christians. A few come from the urban middle class. Almost all of us are younger than twenty. Most women joined the guerrillas after their villages were set on fire by the army, or just before such an attack. Others, because the repression made it impossible to continue working in the city.

Many women saw their parents, brothers and sisters, husbands or children murdered. They were forced to flee for their lives, walking long distances, without food or water, with their children in their arms, dying of dehydration.

Many things are difficult for women: hard work, stern discipline, scarcity of water. Often, we can't bathe when we are menstruating. We have no sanitary napkins. It's hard to get enough to eat, sanitation is terrible. We get malaria (with high fevers and shivers) from time to time, or anemia, parasites, mountain leprosy, painful skin diseases or malnutrition.

We must always be alert, prepared for an unexpected confrontation with the army. Women guerrillas learn a lot, from how to swing a machete and how to make tortillas, to how to detonate mines, stage ambushes, take hostages and shoot well. On top of this, there is the complicated science of leading a collective and administering production.

To organize the war better, work is specialized. There are combatants, radio operators, health workers (we call them "witches"), compañeras who work in agricultural production, political commissioners and so on. We all take turns with security, kitchen duty, gathering firewood, carrying corn and more. We get up at dawn, or before, depending on the situation and the tasks to be done. We quickly pack our equipment into our backpacks — a hammock, tent, mosquito netting and sometimes a blanket. Of course, collecting everything quickly doesn't always work. Sometimes the knot on the hammock gets stuck, or the mosquito nets get tangled; then you hear people swearing.

The head of the camp tells us whose turn it is to do kitchen duty, gather firewood, which patrol will be going out on a mission, when a study group will meet and so on. Then we have breakfast — tamales or tortillas. How much we eat depends on the amount of corn. Sometimes we get one big tortilla or three little ones for each meal.

Eugenia is a "witch." Today she's on kitchen duty with Luis. They get up very early in the morning. Eugenia lights the fire. Luis washes the *nixtamal*,[10] holding the lantern in his mouth. He scrubs hard with both hands, as if he were washing clothes. Next he grinds the corn. Eugenia puts the *comal*[11] over the fire, grabs a little ground corn, adds water and kneads it. Now she can start making tortillas. They have to be of a certain size and thickness, perfectly round, the edges all the same. You have to learn to make them and turn them in total darkness. They must come out white and not burned.

Rosalia is a radio operator. She's Cakchiquel. She's always smiling and singing. She likes romantic songs. Today it's her turn to collect firewood, and with her rifle on her shoulder and her machete in hand she leaves the camp. Half an hour later she returns with her third of the firewood carried gracefully on her head. She dumps it on the ground in the kitchen and starts speaking Cakchiquel with Artemio.

In the jungle it rains a lot, and since we are generally on the move, we get wet. The fire — made only at night — dries us, our backpacks, our bullets and gives us light to prepare the corn. On the coldest nights, the fire helps keep us warm, although the *compas* say the best thing is to share your hammock with another body.

Four men and three women go out to harvest corn. The patrol leader tells us to be alert — we shouldn't leave any trace of our passing — and finally what to do in case we meet the enemy.

It rained a lot the night before, and we have to make our way through a lot of mud. We meet with an alligator while crossing a pond, and we take him with us for supper. We walk peacefully, breathing the pure air, listening to bird songs. Our backpacks are light because we're carrying only our equipment. The way back will be a different story.

We arrive. The sun hurts our eyes. We divide up the tasks and talk about security. We go to work. At night we eat a little alligator with tortilla. Then we prepare the corn we'll take the next day. We shuck the corn and remove the grain and fill our backpacks. Each of us will carry between thirty and one hundred pounds.

We go to sleep exhausted, sweaty and very thirsty. Early the next day we start the journey home. I put on a *mecapal*[12] to carry my backpack. It's excellent: you feel like you're carrying nothing on your shoulders. The work is done with your head, which hurts horribly for the first half hour. Then I feel better. I walk mechanically, thirsty and sweating a lot.

When we get back to camp, it's rest time, and that means a bath! I take two buckets of water, cut six *guano*[13] leaves and stand over them, enjoying the water. We use soap when we have it. The only thing that interrupts this pleasure is that you can never let your guard down, in case the enemy comes. Then there are the horseflies and the mosquitoes — if it weren't for these things, it would be perfect.

Anita and her *compa*, Rubén, are rare among the guerrillas. They love one another and are about to have a child. Everything is lived intensely during war, including love. It's very difficult to maintain a relationship. Work separates couples, sending them different places. On the other hand, there are few women and many men. Everyone longs to have a partner, but it isn't possible in our situation. But we are resigned. No woman can be happy if her sister, friend or any other woman has children who die of hunger or who are murdered by repressive forces.

Anita is at the end of her pregnancy. The army is close by, and she has to walk quickly for kilometres and kilometres, climbing up and down steep hills covered with thick vegetation, until she finds a place to have her baby.

One morning the "witches" order everyone to stay away from the area where Anita is. Soon we will have a new combatant. We are very anxious, hoping that everything will be easy. I can't help worrying. What if the baby dies? What if she needs a cesarean? What will we do? Happily, at eight in the morning a precious child is born. We go and see the little boy; he looks like his father. He's asleep, unaware of the war. We take turns holding him in our rough hands. Some cry. In general, there's great happiness.

I've tried to give a quick glimpse of women's lives in the guerrillas. We're like all other women. We like to fix ourselves up, to be pretty. We long to love a compañero, to be mothers. We've taken up arms because that's the continuation of the political process by other means.

I Know Our Struggle is Just and Necessary

Laura, URNG

I'm Laura. I'm twenty-nine years old. I'm *ladina*. I'm going to talk about how I happened to join the revolutionary movement and about some of the experiences I've had during the time that I've been part of it.

A lot of things motivated me to join the struggle. But one of them was the life I had as a girl. I'm from the capital and my family was working-class. My parents were workers and I have five brothers and sisters. I'm the oldest, and I could study only because of my mother's sacrifices. My father drank and they separated when I was small. Soon Mom had to work to support my brothers and sisters and me.

So one motivation was my childhood, all the poverty. Then I was a student and I began to learn more about the situation of workers. After primary school I began to work too, to help my family. I studied and I worked.

Soon after I finished my studies, I began to work as a teacher. I continued studying and joined the students' movement when I was nineteen years old. That was in 1977. And I began to learn a little more about what was happening to our people, about the exploitation of workers, about the repression in the countryside. At the time, the grassroots movement was growing, and many students and unionized workers were being kidnapped and murdered.

Along with the experience I was gaining in the students' movement, I began to have contact with compañeros who worked in campesino organizations. In 1978, I began to work with campesinos. This brought me in closer contact with the exploitation and the oppression our people had been living with for many years, and I began to wake up to the need to participate in our people's liberation. Soon, in 1980, I took up arms as a member of the EGP.[14]

My compañero at the time was also in the EGP. He'd been in the struggle for a longer time. The situation had gotten a lot worse. The Spanish Embassy Massacre had taken place and the repression was more intense in the Highlands and in other parts of the country.

At the end of 1980 my compañero was kidnapped. Up to now, we don't know where he is. What is known is that he was captured by the army — that was proven — and taken to the base in Huehuetenango. It's certain the man was tortured. At the time, I already had one child, born three months earlier. I had to go into hiding. Although it was very painful for me, it never made me question what I was doing. There were difficult times. I had to face being alone with my son. But with the help of my compañeros, I managed. What had happened pushed me forward to fight for the ideals my compañero died for.

I continued working in the front on the south coast, and soon after, I began to work more directly in the EGP. The counter-offensive had begun. The enemy launched its offensive with the scorched earth policy,[15] the burning of villages, the kidnappings of compañeros, kidnappings of entire families.

That was happening in 1980, 1981, 1982. It was a very difficult period in our struggle and for our organization. I've seen burned villages. I know what it is to live with the constant fear that the enemy is right behind us — the roadblocks on the highways, when the army takes everyone off the bus and searches the bus, looking through your belongings, trying to find guerrillas. Where I was, the army came and burned villages and people. They closed the roads and they came in and tortured pregnant women, their children. They came in machine-gunning entire families in some villages.

At the end of 1981, the enemy tried to kidnap me, but I managed to escape. I felt many things at the moment the enemy had me, but I managed to escape, and that was another victory. Soon after that happened I went to work on another front.

Then in 1986 I began to work on the Comandante Ernesto Guevara front. When I got there, the enemy was re-launching the counter-offensive it had more or less stopped in 1985. Then in September 1987 the "Year-End Counter-Offensive" began.

The army came up all the trails to clean us out, with heavy bombardment, like never before. As well as cannons, they were using helicopters armed with rockets. September, October and November were very difficult. I'd never lived through bombings and machine-gunnings of that kind. Not that level of bombing. Thirty or forty bombs at a time. It was terrible. You feel fear and courage when you see them throwing everything they have at you, trying to finish you off. Our morale was very high.

We had to withdraw with compañeras who were sick, with children, with pregnant compañeras, with those who had recently given birth, with their belongings too — their clothes, pots, all the animals. We withdrew when the enemy was getting close. During almost the entire counter-offensive, we managed to avoid the enemy.

But during all this we had some very difficult moments. A helicopter right over us, trying to find us. Watching how they fired — as if they wanted to vent their rage. We were there under the trees, just waiting to see what was going to happen. Nothing happened. The enemy couldn't achieve anything. Under the bombing we had to go on working, bringing in the harvest. There we were, with the enemy telling us to surrender, that we were being tricked. But nothing came of it. We didn't pay any attention.

During that counter-offensive, I had to live through the death of my second compañero. We'd been living together for five years, and my compañero was killed in action. The enemy bombed and my compañero died in the bombardment.

It affected me deeply. Like me, many compañeras have lost compañeros they loved very much, worthy compañeros because every one gave something important. That hurt me a lot, but I got solidarity and support from my compañeros in the struggle, and that has given me the strength to go on.

The second stage of the counter-offensive, "Strength '88," put battalions against our front. The initial tactics of the first counter-offensive didn't work. That forced them to change their plans and launch another offensive. But in every skirmish we brought down ten or fifteen soldiers.

The bombardments and the machine-gunnings haven't weakened me. On the contrary, they have strengthened me. I know our struggle is just and necessary to liberate our people.

Hope is the Last to Die

Ines, URNG

I'm from the central Highlands. My name is Ines. When the space for struggle begins to disappear, you decide to join another kind of struggle. You decide to take arms. It's the only way in Guatemala. In the beginning you work, wanting to bring change another way. But there's no longer any other way. You're left thinking: What are we going to do? We can't demonstrate any more. You realize this is the only way. That's when I decided to give myself entirely to the revolutionary movement, to the armed struggle.

Before it was very hard to work with Indigenous women, to help them see there was no other way. Many of them were married. Many were young — their parents wouldn't let them participate. But as a result of the repression, many Indigenous women have joined the revolutionary movement.

My own experience is that it's very easy for Indigenous women to join because our life in the countryside has been collective. There's not much individualism because we all have the same problems. That's where I didn't feel much of a change.

When we first were talking about it my husband didn't want to join. He said we should continue to work as we had before. But I told him we couldn't work that way anymore. I insisted and insisted and in the end he understood.

It's been different for me in the sense that not only the women work, but the men too. They help the women. Many women have had to go into the mountains with their children to join the guerrillas. Everyone there helps with the child. He or she isn't just the mother's child. One person takes care of the child one day; another person, the next. This makes taking care of the child easier for the mothers.

The compañeros aren't like they were in civilian life, where they did as they liked and the women often had to do everything. It's totally different. Everyone works. Women's work is recognized. It has been a little difficult for the men, but they've changed a lot. Before they were used to women doing everything, and here they have to wash their clothes, cook their food. They have to do everything. It's not just the women.

For me this has been very important. This is part of what women are fighting for. That everyone works, not just the women in the kitchen or with the children.

We all have our jobs to do. Of course, we aren't going to say that the women are no longer going to make tortillas. That would be a mistake. But now work is shared because the women often have something to do. And when they return, it's their turn in the kitchen. The next day they go somewhere else. It isn't just men. It isn't just women. Now everyone has work to do, and they help each other.

We've always said that hope is the last to die. We hope that change is coming soon because it's already been too long. We need change, not just the women in the countryside but all working-class women, Indigenous women and poor *ladinas*, because we all suffer exploitation, repression and discrimination. But more than anything we Indigenous women have never been accepted anywhere. We've seen it, felt the pressure. That's our struggle.

According to our history, it wasn't always like that. Before, women were treated differently. Women were valued more because we are the bearers of children. Now it's not like that. Now women aren't worth anything. And this has its roots in the arrival of the Spaniards, in the Conquest. That's really where this exploitation, this repression comes from. Not only for women, but for men too. I think that's where this — and I don't like the word — machismo, comes from. They always say that women don't work, but nonetheless at home there's a lot of work with the children, with all you have to do in the home. The men don't participate because they're at work all day. If women had access to other kinds of work, we could take turns. Women could work in a different way, participate in a different way. That's what we're struggling for.

Endnotes

1. Interview with a member of the URNG, February 1990.
2. Ernesto Guevara, *Guerrilla Warfare/Che Guevara* (Lincoln: University of Nebraska Press, 1985), p. 133.
3. URNG, *Unitary Proclamation of the Guatemalan National Revolutionary Unity*, January 1982.
4. Castillo Armas was a former colonel and the U.S.– selected front man for the coup that toppled the Arbenz government.
5. Castillo Armas was killed by one of his personal guards in 1957, in what may have been a power struggle within the National Democratic Movement (MDN), his far-right political party.
6. In 1953, Fidel Castro led a failed raid on the Moncada army barracks.
7. *Compa*: compañero.
8. By 1991 the URNG was operating in fourteen depart-

ments, including three not mentioned by Judith: Alta Verapaz, Santa Rosa and Sacatepéquez.

9. Excerpted and translated from the guerrilla newspaper published by the FAR, *Guatemala en lucha*, 8 March 1987, pp. 6–15.

10. *Nixtamal*: corn soaked and boiled in lime, ready to be ground.

11. *Comal*: clay griddle used for frying tortillas.

12. *Mecapal*: head band used for carrying heavy load.

13. *Guano*: a variety of palm.

14. EGP: Guerrilla Army of the Poor.

15. Search and destroy operations levelling everything in the path of the military.

Afterword

My Mother Will Be With Us
for Hundreds of Years

Rigoberta Menchú,[1]
Campesino Unity Committee

These days I've been remembering my home, and I realize there are riches in that way of life that have never been collected anywhere. Sadly, with the passing of time, many values are being lost.

I don't know how we survived; there were so many children. Each of us had to find a way to survive from a very young age. Like all the poor in Guatemala, we had to do many things to stay alive. It wasn't just going to the plantations, or doing small jobs, or working with the neighbours. I remember going to the river to look for mussels, for plants, for mushrooms and taking them from one village to another to sell for a few pennies.

When one of my sisters was six months old, my father was jailed for the first time, and my mother had to leave her with us. My mother went to work as a servant in the capital, Santa Cruz del Quiché. We would have been around six or seven years old; the oldest was twelve or thirteen. She left my little sister with us, and we had to take her to an aunt who lived about half an hour away, to be nursed. She had a baby almost the same age. But my aunt was poor too, and she didn't have much free time. So we could only take my sister once or twice a day to nurse. The rest of the time my sister was nursed by a goat. My mother was gone for almost a year. My father was in jail. When my mother returned my sister was dying.

On top of this: being forced to pick coffee and cotton on the coast beneath a sun so endless it scorches. Coming from the Highlands where it's muddy and cold, only to land on the coast with an endless sun, was an enormous change. It's very cold in the Highlands, especially from January to March.

For many years, our community has had a very collective way of organizing. Men or women who become leaders don't get their authority through laws or just because of their record. It depends on their work, sacrifice, dedication. It takes a lot of work to gain our people's affection and respect. Leaders begin to earn this at an early age. My father was a leader for many years and my mother too.

From the time we're young, we're taught to respect our elders. When we see older people in the village, we greet them with a very special gesture. It's the greeting given to an uncle, an aunt or a mother.

This strong, deep, collective life begins in the way our people think about birth, the family, pregnancy, conception. And above all, about nature.

A few days ago, I was remembering some very old legends. There's Juajiup, the Owner of Nature. It's a beautiful concept, part of our life, our teaching about respecting nature. I don't know if it's a legend because many people believe they've seen the Enchanter, the Owner of Nature. When men have caused great destruction, great harm to nature, Juajiup might appear at anytime. But they say that he appears as nature's most beautiful animal. He could appear as a little rooster, one never seen before, or as a lovely bird. He appears to special people, the ones with the greatest gifts. You have to have merit to see this animal. All this animal does is show itself. You must not grab it or follow it. You must carry the message to the community. It means the Owner of Nature is worried because men are causing great destruction.

We know this teaching from the time we're very young. Whenever I'm in the mountains, I remember it. It's part of life, taking care of nature.

Such moments happen every day in our communities. There are very moving moments, collective acts where we blend the Christian religion, the Mayan religion and our customs. Holy Week, for instance, is the only day of the year you pay a visit to all your neighbours. Our neighbours bring us something, and we give to the others.

It's the only time of year bread is eaten. You make a little bread, and you give some of it — even if it's just a little piece — to your neighbours. And they give you a little bread, with a little syrup from sugar cane, or dark sugar. At midday, you make some special tortillas — white tortillas, made with white corn — and white beans. Then the whole neighbourhood exchanges food. We had the most wonderful time. My brothers and sisters and I would choose where we wanted to go and leave bread or leave tortillas. It's a big job taking three or four tortillas to every neighbour — there were about sixty families in the neighbourhood.

There are other celebrations too: births, baptisms, planting celebrations. When work begins in January or February, people have beautiful gatherings, planting ceremonies. Soon after, we celebrate the seed ceremonies. All planting ceremonies are very important. There are wedding ceremonies too.

What comes out of this is continuity. Nobody breaches this unless they go far away for a long time. Then sometimes they lose all this.

My mother was a hardworking woman, with nine children. But all her life, both in the Highlands and on the coast, she devoted herself to being a midwife. She was a midwife from age sixteen until her death at fifty-three. She was a midwife and a healer who knew medicinal plants. Really, she was the doctor for many, many communities close to the village. And she didn't earn one penny; it was all voluntary work. Later, when she went to the coast, it was the same. Many women had their children on the plantations, and my mother helped them. My mother became very well known. Most people in my generation called her Grandma because she was the godmother, the midwife.

She used to tell a beautiful story from her childhood. My grandfather never liked to keep pigs; he thought pigs were dirty animals that shouldn't be kept in the house. My grandfather was a very traditional man, very old. He died in 1979, when he was 119. My mother found a little pig halfway up the mountain when she went to herd the sheep. She brought the little pig home with her and hid him in the *temazcal*.[2] It was there for a long time, without my grandfather noticing. When she went to herd the sheep, she took the little pig along, and when she came back she would hide it in the *temazcal* again.

But one day my grandfather noticed and he told my mother, "This animal shouldn't be in our house. It's dirty. If you don't get rid of it, I'm going to kill it." After that, my mother left it in the corral with the sheep. Two or three weeks went by, with my grandfather constantly criticizing the pig.

One night coyotes came. When they heard the coyotes,

they let the dogs loose. The coyotes went in the corral and the only thing they carried off was the pig. So many sheep — and they took the pig. My mother says she saw the coyotes carrying the pig up the hill. It was an important lesson for her. She never believed they were really coyotes.

Another time, after she was married, she got lost in the mountains, near the village of Chimél where we used to live. My oldest brother had been born only a few weeks earlier. She had gone down to the river to wash my brother's diapers. Suddenly, she felt she'd lost her vision. She got up and she saw lovely *pacayas*,[3] precious doves, flowers. She wanted to go home, but she couldn't find the path. When she went one way, it was blocked by thorns. She went another way and it was the same. She felt as if only an hour had passed, but it was an entire day. The diapers turned up in the river, but she didn't. My father had to alert the neighbours. They took my brother somewhere else to nurse, and they raised a ruckus. At seven in the evening, my mother appeared, close to home. She thought it was eight in the morning.

She talked a lot about good and evil — it's almost the same as the parts of the *Popul Vuh*,[4] that talk of Xibalbá, the Evil One. People know the *Popul Vuh* not as a book but as oral history. Many things aren't told in books, but people talk about them in our language. They tell great stories, but they aren't written down any place. I remember many, many legends. I try to remember them as my grandparents told them. Maybe someday they'll be important in preserving our values.

Among ourselves, we talk about our ancestors, about creation, about nature, but not exactly about Ixmucané. But we talk about Grandmother Moon, Mother Earth, Father Sun. Above all, Mother Earth. For us, the earth has never been just an economic resource. It's the source of life, the reason for being. It isn't just where we grow corn.

In other places, especially among the Cakchiquel, the Tzutuhil, people have preserved even more. And where there are more *aj-k'ij*,[5] there are many more Mayan priests who preserve all this. For us, there are no longer Mayan priests, as such. There were the Ajkmajke, the guides or leaders. Not just the leader, but the one who clears the way on the path — that little word has a lot of meaning. My father was an Ajkmajke. My mother too, but above all my father, because his struggle was an economic, political and cultural one.

A few women have become leaders. My mother had the gift of being a midwife. And she was a bold woman who forged ahead, no matter what the problem. People value that. You have to have a gift to be a leader. This isn't to say that women aren't valuable; just that most places the leaders are men.

Now, with the economic struggle and the struggle for land, women have become much more involved. Before, women weren't involved. Women were never listened to. She wasn't taken into account inside organizations, nor could she become a political leader — more than just a local leader or a cultural leader. This has changed in recent years.

The destruction of my family and my community is something so terrible. The collective memory of our area was destroyed. We grew up with a very particular way of life. We were very poor, but at the same time, we were very close to nature. Our way of life is very difficult to express in words. Perhaps no one thought someday someone would try to oppose it. We were part of nature — there was no reason to destroy it.

In the end our home, our family and our history were shattered. We had to leave. And that's when family ties began to be broken. Even the animals felt this. My mother told me that at a certain point, all the bees being kept in our house left. Our community believes the family bees are very sacred — bees will only live with an upright family, an honest family, a happy family. When we left the house and the family broke up, the bees began to go away in groups.

It was a very difficult world to have to break away from. But afterwards, it was even more difficult to accept what had happened. You are born into a certain way of life, and now no sign of it remains.

Of my nine brothers and sisters, only three of us are alive — my two youngest sisters and I. Two brothers disappeared. I still think maybe they'll appear someday. The others were murdered, including my parents.

It was terrible to find out our parents were burned alive.[6] They were such good people. I knew the compañeros who were killed at the Spanish Embassy — all were such good people with dreams for the future. Maybe it was better that they weren't around to see what happened afterwards.

In my mother's case, little by little, we reconstructed what happened. It took about two or three years for my brothers and sisters and me to collect clues one by one. And finally, when we put the information together, we knew our mother had been tortured, raped. She has no grave, though she was very loved and respected. No one could risk collecting her body because it would have been too dangerous.

Many of our friends and family fled and lived for four or five years in the mountains, without blankets, without clothes, without anything. They came back to the village and found traces of things and then went off again. The army came in and occupied the village time and time again. Finally, they began to do sweeps with four or five thousand men. That's how many people who weren't killed in the massacre of 1982 ended up dying in the mountains.

In 1983, many people were picked up in one of the offensives. They took them down to the village and killed them. Few survived. They killed my brother Victor in the village. He had five children. They killed his wife. They killed his children — maybe one is alive, but they killed the older ones and the babies.

The community doesn't exist any longer. The army has turned it into a cattle ranch. One of those landowners who was always on the lookout for an abandoned community came and occupied it. It makes me furious every time I think about the village. And it hurts me that a land so loved by its people and so well cared for is being destroyed. With a cattle ranch, the land erodes in a few years.

I remember my grandfather making his coffin and my grandmother's too. My grandmother helped. This was six years before my grandfather's death and three years before my grandmother died. After they finished their coffins, they stored them up in the rafters until my grandmother died. My grandfather loved his coffins: he cleaned them and kept them covered so they wouldn't get dirty. Death was expected and accepted — that's how the old ones died. But this way of thinking about death is shattered when you see a body tossed over a cliff, mutilated, toothless or headless. Many of them were children who'd never done anything. All of them innocent. What's saddest is knowing this has happened in many places.

So much is being lost: weaving, *trajes*, beliefs, collective life, ways of leadership, ways of organizing. It could be society will pay a very high price for this. But then I remember what we're creating. The refugees in the mountains, for instance, have a society many of us dream of — a society where respect is practiced, collective life is practiced, pride of race and ethnic consciousness are practiced. You can see it. People's thinking is so advanced that I think it could create a very human society if it were done on a larger scale. These are values born in the struggle, and of course with a lot of sacrifice.

Despite the military, there is a vast tapestry of hope. Even the army itself can't predict just what the future will bring. Our people are like the jungle, hiding many things within it. That's what makes it possible for us to organize.

The army continues its attacks, its terror tactics, because it knows there is something great within us. No one knows the depth of revolutionary convictions within the people. Not even the army knows how deep it goes. It is incalculable.

One compañero told me, "There isn't a people anywhere who can be held prisoner for so many years... We, the Indigenous people, aren't prepared to live another five hundred years without putting an end to oppression. We're tired of it all. And we never lose hope."

Despite the repression against our organization — many brothers and sisters have died — here we are, stronger than ever. Many women who had never been politically active are taking part. I really feel happy to see so many compañeras working, holding back nothing. In every corner of Guatemala there are daughters and sons who are never going to let us down. There are CUC members whose parents were founders, whose children are involved. And now the grandchildren continue.

One day I was thinking about my mother. There were many mothers like her: so simple, so humble, so real. We hold her and other compañeras who've fallen in very high esteem. It wasn't at all easy for my mother to say, "Fine, today we're all at risk. But each must go where destiny calls." My sister went into the mountains. I went into the CUC. My brothers joined the Communities of the Population in Resistance, in the mountains. Others were kidnapped. For a mother to say, "My children, follow your destiny," took a lot of courage because she stayed with the community until her death.

A little while ago, one of my sisters was reminding me that Mama always said that for Indigenous peoples to leave their land would mean they'd be like orphans, without a future. She was a very traditional woman. My mother was a healer and a midwife — you could say she was really a Mayan Priestess. With her experience and her history, she'll be with us for hundreds of years. She always prayed to the earth, prayed to the land, prayed to the flowers, prayed to the countryside. And to life.

I believe it was the same for many mothers, especially for traditional mothers. For them, leaving the earth meant being orphaned. To keep from being orphaned they had to stay and see what happened. Juana Tun de Menchú: *presente!*

Endnotes

1. Rigoberta Menchú's oral history was published in 1984. See Elisabeth Burgos-Debray, ed., *I... Rigoberta Menchú: An Indian Woman in Guatemala*, trans. Ann Wright (London: Verso, 1984).
2. *Temazcal*: bathhouse. In the Highlands, many people take steambaths rather than tub baths or showers.
3. *Pacayas*: maguey.
4. *Popul Vuh*: sacred writings of the Maya.
5. *Aj-k'ij*: the Time Keeper, the person in charge of maintaining the Mayan calendar. Also, a diviner, one who is responsible for interpreting dreams and advising the community's elders.
6. Rigoberta Menchú's father, Vicente Menchú, was killed in the Spanish Embassy Massacre.

Notes on Contributors

Chapter One

JUANA VÁSQUEZ, a Quiché woman, is a former Roman Catholic nun and a member of the international representation of the Campesino Unity Committee, the largest peasant organization in Guatemala. Vásquez is a member of the team coordinating the campaign on the five-hundredth anniversary of the invasion of the Americas.

MARÍA TERESA AGUILAR is Cakchiquel. She lives in the Quetzal Edzná refugee camp in Campeche, Mexico. She is the only woman member of the Permanent Commission of Guatemalan Refugees in Mexico. Aguilar is the natural mother of five children and the adoptive mother of six.

MARÍA CELESTINA BALÁN, a Cakchiquel woman, is from the department of Chimaltenango and is a member of the Campesino Committee of the Highlands.

PAULA CARMELITA, a Jacalteca woman, is a member of the Ixcán Settlers' Committee of the Communities of the Population in Resistance. She has lived in the jungles of Ixcán in northern El Quiché since 1981, when the members of several cooperatives were forced to flee the advancing army.

ANA ISABEl, a Cakchiquel, is a widow and the mother of two children. She lives in a community of widows and orphans in Guatemala.

Chapter Two

JULIA ESQUIVEl, a *ladina* poet and theologian, was trained as a Presbyterian minister but was never given a ministry. In exile since 1980, Esquivel has lived in Switzerland, Nicaragua and Mexico.

SISTER EUGENIA, a *ladina*, is a Roman Catholic nun and has worked inside Guatemala and in exile.

MOTHER FRANCISCA, an Indigenous woman, is the mother superior of a Catholic religious order in El Quiché. Part of the exodus of Catholic orders from the region in 1980, she returned to El Quiché in 1985.

Chapter Three

MARÍA ISABEL CHOXÓM LÓPEZ, a member of the board of directors of the Mutual Support Group for the Families of the Disappeared (GAM), is also a social worker. Choxóm, a *ladina* of Quiché ancestry, works in a project in one of Guatemala's squatters' settlements.

MERCEDES GÓMEZ, a *ladina*, has lived in exile with her three children since her husband's murder in March 1985.

MARIELA, a Quiché woman, began to work with the Runujel Junam Council of Ethnic Communities after her brother, suffering severe emotional problems because of the war and the repression, was forced to participate in the Civil Patrols.

EMILIA GARCÍA, a *ladina*, is a founding member of GAM.

LINDA NEOMÍ, a young Cakchiquel woman, works in GAM's literacy and weaving programs.

MARÍA, a Quiché woman, is from the department of the same name and works with GAM.

Chapter Four

Labour lawyer MARTA GLORIA TORRES lives in exile and is a member of the United Representation of the Guatemalan Opposition (RUOG), a five-person team, which, among other things, represents the Guatemalan opposition at sessions of the United Nations. She is *ladina* and the mother of five children.

ROSA ESCOBAR, a *ladina*, is a founding member of the Women's Committee of the International Union of Food and Allied Workers' Associations in Guatemala. Escobar is the mother of seven children, three of her own, and four adopted after her sister died in childbirth.

CARMEN GARCÍA, a *ladina*, is a member of her union's executive and a member of the Women's Committee of the International

Union of Food and Allied Workers' Associations in Guatemala.

PATRICIA, a *ladina* single mother, is one of several hundred women who occupied her *maquila* workplace, a garment factory manufacturing the brand names Liz Claiborne and WillyWear, after the owners shut the plant down during a union drive.

THELMA, a *ladina* widow and union activist, also works with the Women's Committee of the International Union of Food and Allied Workers' Associations in Guatemala.

Chapter Five

ROSALINA TUYÚC, a Cakchiquel woman from Chimaltenango, is a widow. She is the co-ordinator of the Board of Directors of CONAVIGUA.

MARÍA MORALES JORGE, a young, single Quiché woman, was one of the initiators of CONAVIGUA.

GRUFEPROMEFAM, the Women's Group for the Betterment of the Family, was one of the first of the new women's groups to appear. GRUFEPROMEFAM's major goals are to defend the rights of working women, and to encourage women's participation in grassroots organizations.

TIERRA VIVA WOMEN'S GROUP, formed in 1988, is one of the first Guatemalan feminist groups.

Chapter Six

CATALINA, a *ladina* who grew up in a wealthy home in Guatemala, was drawn to the revolutionary movement because a brother she loved very much had joined. Today she is a leader in the examination of the situation of women in the revolutionary movement.

JUDITH is from a *ladina* working-class family which had strong ties to the Arbenz government. She has worked as a member of the URNG in Guatemala and abroad.

Women from the Rebel Armed Forces (URNG).

LAURA is a *ladina* woman from a working-class family in Guatemala City, member of the URNG.

INES is a Cakchiquel woman, a widow, and the mother of four children, member of the URNG.

Afterword

RIGOBERTA MENCHÚ, a Quiché woman, is one of Guatemala's better-known spokespersons in exile, a member of the Campesino Unity Committee, and a member of the United Representation of the Guatemalan Opposition.

5468